AMERICAN EAGLES

THE 101ST AIRBORNE ASSAULT ON FORTRESS EUROPE 1944/45

CHARLES WHITING

ESKDALE PUBLISHING

BRITISH LIBRARY CATALOGUING PUBLICATION DATA:
CATALOGUE RECORD FOR THIS BOOK AVAILABLE FROM THE
BRITISH LIBRARY

ISBN 0-9538677-2-2

FIRST PUBLISHED IN THE UK IN 2001 BY
ESKDALE PUBLISHING
ESKDALE HOUSE
46 ST OLAVES ROAD
YORK
ENGLAND
YO30 7AL

TYPESET BY HINDLEY, CORWEN, DENBIGHSHIRE.
PRINTED AND BOUND IN GREAT BRITAIN BY
MACKAY OF CHATHAM PLC, CHATHAM. KENT

Acknowledgements

Without the expert assistance and kind help of
Graham Hindley this book could not have appeared.

The author would also like to thank Carl Shilleto for his expert input.

Also to my old friend and fellow vet. Tom Dickinson
of the New York Public Library system
who as always was a great help.

Charles Whiting
York 2001

Contents

THE INTRODUCTION

In the spring of 1994, a relatively unknown US script-writer, Robert Rodat, was living in the smallish New Hampshire town of Putney Corners. The script-writer was 'bouncing off ideas for a movie' between himself and the living room while he waited for the birth of his second son.

Every day he would take his son for a walk in the early morning hours in between reading the many new books appearing that Spring to commemorate the 50th anniversary of D-Day. These walks usually ended in the little town square where there was a 'monument to those in the village who died in war dating back to the American Revolution'. One thing in particular struck Rodat. 'In almost every war, there were repeated the last names - brothers who were killed in action'. At that time Rodat felt, 'The thought of losing a son to war is painful beyond description; the thought of losing more than one is inconceivable'.

Perhaps the fact that he had just become a father to a second son gelled the idea of a movie on that particular theme - the loss of two sons and brothers in battle. But now Rodat set to work on a script on the subject, finally deciding to locate it in World War Two.

That spring the 50th anniversary of D-Day was being well publicised as a sentimental-nostalgic occasion to celebrate the fallen and the great victory they had achieved on the landing beaches. But it was also a political issue, too. The newspapers in the States were asking whether President Clinton should really go; after all he was regarded by many US citizens as a draft dodger.[1] What about the host, President Mitterrand of France too? His wartime past was pretty murky. He had actually worked for the Vichy Government and had received a medal from its leader, Marshal Petain. Then there was Chancellor Kohl of Germany, the enemy of that time. He had actually been a member of the Hitler Youth and had helped to man a flak battery outside Frankfurt firing at Anglo-American bombers.

D-Day was in the air. People were talking about the coming event throughout the western world. So in the end Rodat decided to set a screenplay against the exceedingly topical background of 6th June 1944. In essence his movie could be about the official rescue on D-Day of a soldier, whose brother (like so many of the brothers marked on that weathered New England war memorial) had already been killed in action. Thus was born the idea of *Saving Private Ryan*.

But should the soldier-brother character be factual or totally fictional? According to the script-writer's own statement, it was the latter. The background and the inspiration for the film came from many books, newspaper and magazine accounts, archival footage, conversation with veterans and other sources. Rodat insisted that the brother(s) were based not on true characters, whose story in *Ryan* bear a striking resemblance to real brothers who took part in D-Day. His inspiration came from that small New England village war memorial.

In due course, after some eleven drafts, the screenplay of what would become *Saving Private Ryan* was put to Tom Hanks, with the proposal that he could play the leading role. It turned out that Hanks was a 'World War Two buff'. He was interested. Now things started to move fast. Spielberg saw the draft script. He liked it because he, too, was interested in that war. *Schindler's List* had worked so well that he thought that *Private Ryan* might well be a winner, too, especially if he could use the same technique as in the concentration camp movie.

By 1997 a deal had been worked out with Paramount and Spielberg's Dream Works SKG both financing the production. The rest, as the cliché has it, was history ...

Three years later Spielberg and Hanks went to war once more. This time they tackled a much more ambitious project than *Private Ryan*. Not only was the budget much greater - an estimated ninety-three million pounds - but also the time span covered more than a couple of days in June 1944. Instead it was spread over a whole year, 1944-1945, and set the action in five countries; Britain, France, Holland, Belgium and Germany.

Based on the Stephen Ambrose's oral history of a single paratrooper company of the 101st Airborne Division, *The Band of Brothers*, it would be a factual account of those hundred-odd men in their combat career from the Normandy beaches to their final triumph of the capture of Berchtesgaden, Bavaria, the location of Hitler's fabled mountain-top eyrie, 'The Eagle's Nest'.

Naturally Professor Ambrose's account of that year in the lives of Easy Company, 506th Parachute Infantry Regiment, 101st Airborne Division, is not strictly accurate, as he would be the first to admit. 'Easy Company got there first', he writes of the 101st's attack on Berchtesgaden. The US 3rd Division and the French 2nd Armoured of General Leclerc would have had something to say about that.

But of course, Professor Ambrose, who was never a soldier himself and was ten years old when World War Two ended, 'felt (as he wrote himself) it was my task to make the best judgement on what was true, what had been misremembered, what had been exaggerated by the old soldiers telling their war stories... [but] we have come as close to the true story of Easy Company as possible'.

In *American Eagles* it is the author's intention to give an accurate description of the 101st's major operations during the European campaign of '44/45. Instead of confining the story to the memories of just one outfit, it will tell the story of *all* the 'Screaming Eagles', through a brief description of their battles and selected eye-witness accounts of what it was like for individual soldiers, from commanding general to the newest and youngest replacement, plus what can be seen of their passing on those battlefields stretching from the beach to Berchtesgaden over five decades later.

I

THE EAGLES PREPARE

Now there was silence. A moment before the pilot of the slow-moving Junkers 52s half loosed the cables. There had been a slight jerk as the glider pilots had brought up the noses of their machines. This was their form of braking. Now the 'Auntie Jus', as the paras called their towing planes, were banking in slow curves. They were on their way back to their fields around Cologne. All noise died away. Everything this May dawn of 1940 seemed unbelievably calm and peaceful.

The paratroopers are so valuable to me that I am only going to use them if it's worthwhile. The Army managed Poland without them. I am not going to reveal the secret prematurely. The paras are my secret weapon.

ADOLF HITLER TO GENERAL STUDENT, COMMANDER,
THE PARACHUTE DIV. OCTOBER 1939

Below Belgium still slept. Over Liege however, there was a pink glow. It meant the night shifts were still busy in the city's great industrial plants. Beyond the Belgian plain stretching into Northern Plan, Hitler's battle objective was empty of light. The French and the neutral Belgians suspected nothing. The thought cheered the 500 paras in the transports and the gliders greatly. They were going into battle for the first time using a totally new means of reaching the battlefield. They had problems though.

When Germany is in danger, there is only one thing for us. To fight, to conquer, to assume we shall die. From our planes, my friend, there is no return.

BATTLE HYMN OF THE GERMAN PARACHUTE CORPS, 1940

Now it was just before four in the morning. The night sky was beginning to flush a dramatic red. It was like a symbol of the great bloody battle to come: the end of the 'Phoney War' and Germany's dash for greatness in the West.

The nine gliders which formed the core of the air assault formed up into its battle formation. To the rear, Lieutenant Witzig, its Commander, fumed with rage. His glider had been forced to crash land on the German side of the border. Still the eighty-odd men of the German 7th Parachute Division's specially trained parachute-engineer detachment did not know that. As the cream of Nazi Germany's pre-war glider pilots began to bring their flimsy planes down, they thought everything was going according to plan.

Do you think we'll pull it off?... I don't know, comrade, but we'll give 'em one helluva surprise at least.

OBERJAGER HEINZ TO PILOT SCHEITHAUER, 1 MAY 1940

Now with the dawn warmth a light haze was beginning to form below. Still the paras of the 7th Parachute Division, craning their necks to peer down below at an unsuspecting Belgium, could make out their objective. It was Belgium's most modern and most important fortress - Fort Eben Emael. It commanded the junction of the River Maas and the Albert Canal. It had to be taken by an invader. But it was regarded by world military specialists as the most impregnable fortification in the whole of Europe.

Stronger than both the French Maginot Line and the German 'Westwall' (Siegfried Line), it was constructed in a series of concrete and steel underground galleries. Here the gun turrets were protected by a special secret steel manufactured at Liege and were manned by 1,200 selected Belgian troops. Now these eighty-odd paratroopers, leaderless as they were, (though they didn't know it yet) were going to crack this formidable nut and open the door for the Führer's great drive to the West. If they succeeded, Hitler planned to be master of Western Europe within six weeks.

The fortification loomed larger and larger. The pilots started to reduce speed. They applied their flaps and nose brakes. The planes shuddered under the strain. In the first one Sergeant Wenzel, soon to become a German national hero, received and honoured by the Führer himself, yelled, 'Helm auf!'

Swiftly the paras clamped on their rimless helmets. They took up the prescribed landing position. The hiss of the wind grew louder. The fuselage trembled. There was first angry snap-and-crackle of small arms fire, a rending crash. Men were flung on all sides. The shrill squeal of skids. The gliders skimmed, bumping and jolting, shedding bits and pieces of metal and canvas as they headed towards the low concrete fort.

The door of the first plane was flung open. The paras stumbled out, running to left and right, crouched low. A Belgian machine gun opened. Orders were rapped out in fast French and slower, more guttural Flemish.[2] The battle had been joined by the hopelessly surprised Belgians. It was five o'clock on the morning of 10th May 1940. 'The Hunter from the Sky', the German 'Fallschirmjager' had commenced the world's first large scale airborne attack.

The surprise attack on Eben Emael and the conquest from the air by General Student's 7th German Parachute Division rocked the Western military establishment. Ten thousand men had done what normally it took a whole army to do in a matter of days instead of weeks. Immediately voices were raised asking that the two great democracies should have similar shock formations, which landed from the sky. Churchill asked for the immediate formation of 5,000 British paratroopers, the future 'Red Devils', who, that June sixty years ago from now, had not a single transport, glider or piece of airborne equipment available, save for a couple of German smocks and the odd parachute.

It was no different in the still neutral America, some three thousand odd miles away from the scene of the action. In those days the US Army was still starved of cash (only the Commander-in-Chief, for example, possessed an official automobile!) and it ranked twentieth in terms of men and power in the world's armies. Even the Bulgarian Army of 1940 was larger than that of the world's largest democracy!

But the powers in Washington made an attempt. Under the command of two junior officers, Lieutenants William Ryder and James Bassett, a 'Parachute Platoon' was established at Fort Benning. The date was 26th June 1940, a date honoured by the thousands upon thousands of US paratroops, who would be proud to wear the metal wings of the US Parachute Regiment. Weeks later, the volunteers from the 29th Infantry Regiment were already jumping from their parachute towers (some of the first trained at the civilian towers of the 1939 World Fair). On August 16th and 19th the first 'paras' sprang from B-18 bombers in the first 'mass jumps' and duly impressed the assembled brass. One month later the US First Parachute Battalion was formed under the command of Colonel 'Bill' Miley, who one day would lead his men of the US 17th Airborne Division in the great jump across the Rhine of March 1945. In that First Battalion there would be the men, officers and NCOs, who would become famous in the annals of their regiment: Sink of Berchtesgaden, Cole, the parachutists' first Medal of Honor winner with the 101st AB in Normandy; Cassidy of Holland etc. Etc. Things were moving fast now.

A Major William Lee, tall, rugged and handsome (of whom we will hear more), took over training and organisation and gained the nickname of 'The Father of the US Airborne Forces', though he was never fated to lead a parachute force into battle. Under his command 'A Provisional Parachute Group' was set up at Fort Benning in March 1941 to continue the rapid expansion of this new, radical and totally untried force.

Two months later the new force got the shot in the arm it needed, though it came from the wrong quarter - the Germans again!

That May, General Student, his forehead still bearing the ugly red scar from the wounds he had received at Rotterdam the year before,[3] pulled off the greatest triumph of any airborne force in the world: he captured the British held island of Crete against determined resistance - and the British Commander, General Freyburg, knew from Churchill that the German paras were coming.[4] As the Army Historical Division put it later: '[It was] the greatest single impetus to US Airborne development and expansion'.

It was. For it showed that airborne operations need not be limited to commando-type raids, such as those being carried out by the British. Operations could be conducted on a large-scale basis, without surface support or ground link-ups (though the Germans did send in mountain troops afterwards to Crete by boat).

Almost at once the single American parachute battalion was ordered to expand into a full, three-battalion strong regiment, the 501st Parachute Regiment. This took place on 10th July that year.

There was no shortage of volunteers for this new and highly dangerous outfit. Thousands passed through the portals of Fort Benning into the parachute school housed in a mixture of wooden huts and tents. The legend over that gate flattered their ego and they believed it implicitly. It read: '**THROUGH THESE PORTALS PASS THE TOUGHEST PARATROOPERS IN THE WORLD**'. Many of them would soon find out they weren't that tough - at first. Still they swarmed forward to be trained, volunteers to the man - and it wasn't the jump pay that attracted them.

> Men joined the paratroopers because they couldn't resist the awful thrill of risking their life in a parachute. They were drawn into the outfit as by a magnet and once in, wouldn't have left if they got the chance. Each man had supreme faith in his ability to take care of himself whatever the odds. For this reason the paratroopers were at times a quarrelsome lot because they could never believe that anybody could beat the hell out of them.
> ROSS C. CARTER, 504 PARACHUTE INFANTRY RGT.

They were all sorts: college boys and men who hadn't reached tenth grade; religious types who never cursed and jailbirds whose every second word was an obscenity... and all were attracted, whatever their background and education, by what one of the earliest volunteers (who survived and many of them didn't) recalled as 'the thrill and adventure of parachute jumping'.

Their first weeks were spent in physical hardening. They might have thought they were tough guys when they entered Fort Benning. Their instructors showed them they weren't; they were 'straight from your momma's titty'. It was the old Army game of breaking a man down before you build him up – 'rebuilt' might have been a better word - in the Army's image.

Reveille at five... nine mile run... tough physical work-out with logs, bags, rocks, etc.... preliminary ground training in parachuting, roll forward, roll backward... and packing parachutes.

Discipline was exceedingly strict. It had to be with volunteers like these men. 'Gimme twenty-five', i.e. twenty-five press-ups, was a standard punishment for minor infringements. NCOs weren't tardy to take on really 'sad sacks' behind the barracks in a bare-knuckle contest. Officers looked the other way. Medics patched up the losers... and no questions were asked.

> We all thought, after this we can take anything they can throw at us.
>
> PRIVATE CHRISTENSON, 101ST AB

In one case, the future Colonel Sink of the 101st Airborne read the Japanese had marched a hundred miles down the Malayan Peninsula to attack Singapore in January 1942. He told his battalion officers, 'My men can do better'. Thus he led his battalion on a one hundred and eighteen mile hike. The weather was horrendous. The first night, it froze and snowed. The temperature fell to a low twenty degrees. The cooking stoves failed to work. The men started out on their second day with fifty miles still to go on bread and jam, not a particularly fortifying diet for infantry who were supposed by the experts to need at least three thousand calories a day.

But they made it. They covered the one hundred and eighteen miles in seventy-five hours, marching at the high speed (for that distance and the terrible weather conditions) of four miles an hour.

> Not a man fell out... but when they fell, they fell face forward.
>
> COL. SINK TO LOCAL ATLANTA PRESS

By January 1942 further expansion had taken place. Four parachute infantry regiments were authorised. The next step was to form

America's first airborne division. For by now Britain, America's new ally, already had two - the 1st and 6th Airborne - and naturally the USA couldn't be seen to be lagging behind the slow-moving tea-drinking 'Limeys'.

In June 1942 the newly promoted 'Father of the Airborne', Brigadier General Lee, was sent to the UK to visit, among other troops, British and Allied airborne formations. He met General Browning, head of the British Airborne, the immaculate former Guards Officer and husband of the best selling female novelist of the day, Daphne du Maurier. He liked 'Boy' Browning and agreed with the founder of the British paratroopers, that America needed a well-organised airborne division like the 1st British Airborne, the 'Red Devils', who would soon have their baptism of fire in North Africa against Rommel.

Back home Lee's suggestions were taken up. Two airborne divisions were to be formed as soon as possible, each composed of two parachute infantry regiments and one glider regiment (non-volunteer). While this was going on, the 2nd Battalion of the US 503rd Parachute Infantry was sent to Britain under the command of Lt. Col. Edson Raff, to join the Red Devils.[5]

On 15th August 1942, the most major move in the history of the US Airborne took place. The 82nd Motorized Division, commanded the year before by General Bradley, one day to be overall land commander of Eisenhower's 12th Army Group in Europe, was split into two. The formation which took on the old division's name and title was the 82nd Airborne Division, 'the All-American', under hook-nosed General Ridgway, soon to be known as 'Iron Tits' on account of his gimmick of carrying a carbine and two grenades on the breast webbing straps of his combat gear. The other and newer outfit was the 101st Airborne, 'The Screaming Eagles', rightly commanded by the 'Father of the Airborne'. The 82nd was now to be stationed at Fort Bragg; the 101st at Claiborne.

The great rivalry between the two elite divisions, which would so often fight side by side in the World War Two battles to come, had commenced. But in one particular, the 'Screaming Eagles' had the edge on the 82nd. General 'Matt' Ridgway had not yet jumped out of an aeroplane. Ridgway - a man of few words - for which many of his officers were grateful, had a hair-trigger temper and a bitter tongue - soon remedied that. He underwent a ten-minute training session and jumped thereafter in short order (he was also one of the first in the 82nd to have a ride in the much criticized WACO glider in order to appease his much maligned glider-borne troops who were drafted into the division and received no jump pay).[6] But throughout his airborne career, Ridgway never did manage to put in more than a minimal five jumps needed to gain his wings.

> I would give a year's pay if the desk-bound son of a bitch in Washington who decided crash landing in one of those canvas coffins isn't hazardous duty would go up with us just once.
>
> ANON. GLIDERMAN OF 82ND AB, 1942

But by 1943, it was clear that the 82nd Airborne was going to beat the rival 101st. It was selected for overseas duty first in a combat zone, sailing for North Africa and the unknown. A little later the 'Screaming Eagles' did the same, bound for Britain and further training (as we shall see).

> We were bivouacked in the desert about two miles from Oujda in French Morocco, hell hole if there ever was one. Five hundred of us lived in pup tents... The desert was hard as rock, our water supply scanty - about a quart of water a day... Millions of flies specked the air. We all got dysentery, known in the Army as the GIs - and other plainer terms.
>
> ROSS CARTER, 82ND AB

Indeed they suffered worse things than the 'squitters'. Broken limbs for one. All their jumps on the hard stony desert seemed to result in scores, sometimes nearly a hundred casualties, through broken limbs and fatalities, too. These jumps were not helped either by the prevailing winds which were too strong for mass jumps - indeed jumps in the States under such conditions would not have been condoned. But in the Middle East, with defeat for Rommel and his 'Afrika Korps' just round the corner, time was running out for the airborne. They and their comrades of the 1st British Airborne had been picked for the boldest and largest airborne operation yet undertaken by the Western Allies.

> We will assault Sicily early in July, with the British 8th Army under General Montgomery attacking the eastern beaches... and the US Seventh Army under General Patton attacking the southern beaches... We will use airborne troops on a much larger scale than has yet been attempted in warfare.
>
> GEN. EISENHOWER TO WAR CORRESPONDENT, 10TH JUNE 1943, ALGIERE

The die had been cast ...

The invasion of Sicily was a success, but only a partial one. The bulk of the German forces managed to escape to the Italian mainland to live and continue the fight for the 'soft underbelly', as Churchill was wont to call it ('tough old gut' was the ordinary footslogger's angry opinion) for another twenty-two months.

The same could be said of the two division airborne invasion. It went wrong from the start. Colonel Gavin's 505th Parachute Infantry Regiment was scattered all over the place (Ridgway, the commander of the 82nd Airborne to which 505th belonged, did not jump). Some say units of the 505th landed as far afield as Greece. Eisenhower, waiting for new of the success of the operation at an airborne field in Malta, was greatly surprised by a sudden glider landing and a young officer setting up a gun position just in front of him. The officer thought he had landed in Sicily!

The British 'Red Devils' fared little better. Their divisional commander's glider was ditched in the Mediterranean due to intense 'friendly fire' which panicked the tow plane pilots of the US Troop Command and was forced - to his intense chagrin and anger - to go into action dressed as a naval steward.[7] But although the airborne men behaved bravely and captured most of their initial objectives, they ended the Battle of Sicily being used as 'straight-legs', i.e. ordinary infantry.

> The great confidence of the troopers in their own ability to do the job was not shared by everyone in higher headquarters. The War Department had observers in headquarters in North Africa during the Sicilian operation... they returned to Washington quite pessimistic. They doubted the concept of an airborne division was valid.
>
> Gen. Gavin, 82nd AB Division

It was an opinion shared by General Eisenhower, the Supreme Commander, who realised that Sicily had not been the world-shaking success he had anticipated. After all it was the first large-scale operation that he had personally commanded. On 20th September 1943, he wrote flatly to General Marshall, the head of the US Army in Washington: 'I do not believe in the airborne division'.

Washington dithered.

For a while, Marshall, who called the tune as far as the Army was concerned, sat on the fence. In the UK, the newly arrived 'Screaming Eagles' of the 101st bitched about the warm beer and tasteless Brussels sprouts and prepared for the Battle of France to come, unaware that they might not be part of that battle. For General McNair, the Army's Commander of US Ground Forces, didn't like the idea of divisional-scale airborne outfits. He was prepared to break up not only the 82nd and 101st, but also the planned 13th and 17th AB Divisions.

> My staff and I have become convinced of the impracticality of handling large scale airborne units... recommended to the War Department that airborne divisions be abandoned... and that the airborne effort be restricted to parachute units of battalion size or smaller.
>
> LT. GEN. L. McNAIR, 1943

The future of the 101st Airborne now began to look decidedly uncertain ...

But suddenly a general more flamboyant than Patton took a hand in the game on the other side of the world. Churchill and the British Chief-of-Staff, who was by no means pro-American (on the contrary, he didn't think much of American general-ship), called this American 'the greatest general and strategist the war has produced'. His men called him 'Dugout Doug'. Naturally they were referring to General Douglas MacArthur, the Allied supremo in the Far East and Pacific.

In September 1943 while the airborne controversy raged in Washington, he decided to retake airstrips in the Japanese-held Australian possession of New Guinea. To do so, MacArthur decided to drop 1,700 paratroops in the Makham Valley near the township of Lae. The valley was one of the few spots in the virtually unexplored terrain of New Guinea where airstrips could be built quickly and easily.

But speed was of the essence, if MacArthur was going to capture the ground before the Japanese counter-attacked in strength. To ensure that his men had the kind of heavy artillery support that Ridgway had lacked in Sicily, 'Dugout Doug' recruited a troop of gunners from the 2/4th Australian Field Artillery Regiment. The surprised 'Aussies' were trained as paras within forty-eight hours while their stripped down 25-pounder cannons were places underneath the transport planes. This was a totally new technique, which would be adopted by all airborne forces over the next few years.

Then MacArthur, a man in his sixties, sprang a surprise on his staff; he was going to accompany the airborne assault! It was as if 'Ike', who had once been MacArthur's young aide before the war, had decided to accompany Colonel Gavin on the attack in Sicily. But then after all, in the First World War, MacArthur had won the Congressional Medal of Honor like his father before him.

> They are my kids and I want to see them do their stuff. But you risk some five-dollar a month Jap aviator shooting a hole through you. I'm not worried about getting shot. Honestly, the only thing that disturbs me is the possibility that when we hit the rough air above the mountains my stomach might get upset. I'd hate to throw up and disgrace myself in front of the kids... But you're right, George. *We'll both go!*
>
> MACARTHUR TO HIS AIR FORCE CHIEF, GEN. GEORGE KENNEY

Minutes after the conversation with Kenney, MacArthur, the most important Allied soldier in the Pacific, took off on the long flight to New Guinea in the Lead Flying Fortress. He didn't allow the pilot to turn back even when one of the transport's four engines failed. So 'Dugout Doug' saved the Airborne. His paratroopers landed safely on the designed DZs and set about capturing their objectives. They did so with few casualties. MacArthur, highly pleased with himself, wired his young wife, who survived him for nearly four decades, 'It was a honey'. Then he set about telling the world ...

> Mine eyes have seen MacArthur with a Bible on his knee
> He is pounding out communiqués for guys like you and me
> And while possibly a rumor now
> Some day 'twill be a fact
> That the Lord will hear a deep voice say,
> Move over, God, it's Mac.
>
> PARODY SUNG TO THE TUNE OF 'THE BATTLE HYMN OF THE REPUBLIC' BY
> PARAS IN NEW GUINEA

Then no-one knew of that parody. All that Washington and Joe Public learned was that MacArthur had actually flown a mission with his paratroopers. Ninety-six transports had successfully dropped 1,700 paras against surprised Jap opposition. Within twenty-four hours US engineers were already building the first of the planned airstrips.[8] MacArthur's publicity machine won the day. The airborne force was saved. In due course the 'All Americans' would return from Italy to prepare for the Invasion of France - and the 'American Eagles', the 101st Airborne Division, would achieve their everlasting glory after all.

II

OLD JOLLY*

*British-born Bob Hope's wartime name for Britain

In June 1942, a tall handsome newly promoted Brigadier General arrived in Britain in the company of other new generals of the US Army, who were destined to become household names. Generals Arnold, Eisenhower, Somervell. The husky Brigadier General belonging to the newest arm of the US Army was, however, fated to disappear into obscurity. This, despite the fact that he had been called 'the Father of the US Airborne'.

He was, as we already know, forty-seven year old William Lee, soon to command one of America's new airborne divisions, and his mission was to find out what role that division could play in the coming invasion of Nazi Europe. He liased, in due course, with his opposite numbers in the British Airborne Forces and those of the Allies, and returned to the States full of enthusiasm for the new weapon. One month later the Pentagon authorised the formation of the 82nd and 101st Airborne Division, both to consist of two glider-borne regiments and one of parachute infantry. Lee, already something of a veteran in airborne affairs, was given command of the latter formation, nicknamed the 'Screaming Eagles' after its divisional patch, the head of the American eagle. One year later, still under the command of General Lee, who wasn't as fit as he looked, it arrived in what British-born Comedian Bob Hope was now calling 'Old Jolly'. The 'Screaming Eagles' had completed the first leg of their two-year journey to war - and glory.

For most of the troopers the transition to war-bound England was strange. Naturally they had already heard of the 'Limeys' delight in stewed tea and Brussels sprouts (they had suffered enough at the hands of British cooks on the long voyage over). But it wasn't just the food or the weather that was strange; it was the way they now lived in the small villages and townships of middle England. Back in the States - 'the land of the round doorknob' - they had been isolated in huge sprawling encampments, the 'forts' that criss-crossed the remoter parts of the country. Here in 'Old Jolly', they lived 'cheek-by-jowl' with 'the natives'.

A few had been placed in hastily evacuated British Army barracks, such as those in Reading. But most lived in village halls, the occasional great house, Nissen huts, barns, even sheds. They filled up the 'olde worlde' villages of Berkshire and Wiltshire - Littlecote, Aldbourne, Chilton Foliat and the like, where live hadn't changed much since the last century.

Here the tough, young, swaggering paratroopers, who believed the world belonged to them, had to contend with such oddities as pubs which served warm beer and not much of that as it was rationed and were closed sometimes by ten at night; vicars and good ladies of the village, who wanted to invite them to spelling bees and 'tea'; strange foods such as fish and chips (soon becoming a popular addition to their diet) and powdered eggs on toast - a whole new world to most of these 12,000 young men dumped down in the middle of slow-moving rural England.

Naturally such young men fated to die sooner or later (or so they believed from their own publicity) wanted to live before they did so. They sought out the big cities to sow their wild oats. They got drunk, they smashed vehicles, they got into race riots, they got into fights with British soldiers, in particular with the Red Berets of the British 6th Airborne Division, also training in the same area for the D-Day landings.

The British were friendly, 'Hello Yank'. 'Got any gum, chum', and all that sort of thing. But we were young and full of piss and vinegar. I think sometimes now fifty years on that we went out of our way to cause trouble. Perhaps it was all due to sex.

Ex-Sgt. S. Smith, 506 PIR

At Devizes in the area occupied by both the 6th British Airborne and the 101st, there was a massive barney between some five hundred Britons and Americans of the two formations. The little country town, in 1944 to be the scene of the mass German POW breakout at the height of the Battle of the Bulge, had never seen anything like it in all its one thousand odd year history. The battling paras fought it between the Market Place and the Corn Exchange for what, to the locals seemed hours, until finally three platoons of Military Police managed to quell the fracas. What had it all been about? National pride? The 'honour of the regiment'? No, just the usual stuff – 'women'.

But for the 101st that winter of 1943/44, with the Allies finally moving over to the attack after Montgomery's victory at El Alamein and the 'Screaming Eagles' sister division, the 82nd Airborne, already having their first taste of combat, first in Sicily and then in Southern Italy, all was not 'cakes and ale'. Their training was becoming progressively harder and more dangerous. For now a lot of it was being carried out, using live ammunition.

The 'Screaming Eagles' trained eight hours a day (or night) six days a week.

They dug their way across middle England, sleeping in foxholes

30

for the first time, those ready-made graves that would undoubtedly be the final resting place for all too many of those keen young men. They advanced under live fire, with an expected ten per cent rate of casualties. They made ever longer route marches - seven - fifteen - finally twenty-five miles at a time. They suffered sprains, broken limbs and sometimes even broken backs, practising judo and unarmed combat against nasty, contemptuous instructors, armed with knives and bars (iron). They established a jump school at the village of Chilton Foliat to qualify the doctors, chaplains, forward artillery observers who would accompany them on the great undertaking as trained parachutists.

Those who didn't make the grade were weeded out. The 101st was carrying no one on D-Day, not even those of exalted rank. That winter 'The Father of the US Airborne', the now Major-General Lee, suffered a heart attack. It must have been a terrible blow for the officer who had worked so hard ever since 1940 to prepare an American airborne unit. Still he had to go just as the lowest Private who hadn't made the grade. Soon he would be dead.

His place was taken by Brigadier Maxwell Taylor, at that time artillery commander of the recently returned 82nd Airborne. Taylor, a West Pointer who would command the 101st until the end of the war, was a strong dominant personality, who would go on to become US Ambassador to Vietnam. But to the rank-and-file, he seemed somewhat remote with little understanding of the lives of the ordinary soldier.

I remember now in Holland or Normandy, I forget exactly which, he told a bunch of us that we'd be glad to know we'd be going into action again on the next day. He thought we'd jump at the chance. We didn't. He was that kind of General.

PFC 'X' OF 506 PIR

Training grew ever more intense. Fist fights and riots grew less frequent. The troopers were too busy - and too exhausted. Now the Brass concentrated on large unit exercises. England was a small country. It was difficult to find terrain and space suitable for a divisional-strong mass drop. But there was the first two battalion-strong jump, the largest so far, with the 2nd and 3rd Battalions of the 506th. Slowly but surely even the thickest trooper began to realise that this was no game. It was a serious business. The war was catching up with them *rapidly*. New Year's Eve 1943/44 came. It was quiet for most of the soldiers. Booze was scarce and perhaps they weren't in the mood to celebrate the advent of the New Year and the deadly uncertainties it brought with it.

We just waited up for the New Year. I wonder what it shall bring, wonder how many of us will see 1945.

GORDON CARSON, 506 PIR

No one could answer the young paratrooper's second question just then. But the answer to his first one had already been decided upon before Christmas. There'd be more training and yet more, but now their training would be checked and approved by the highest authorities in the land. For now the 101st Airborne had been scheduled to be one of the five US elite divisions which would take part in the first day assault on Hitler's vaunted 'Atlantic Wall' and into his 'Festung Europa' (Fortress Europe).

The first 'big shot' to visit the 101st that January in 1944 was no less a person than the 'Victor of El Alamein', General Bernard Law Montgomery, who would command the overall UK/US land operation in Normandy.

It was the standard Montgomery visit. He'd inspected the front ranks of the assembled formation: a cocky little figure, having to look up to most of the troops, a keen, hard look in his blue eyes, set in a wilful face. It was almost as if he were trying to etch each and every face on his mind's eye. At the end of each inspection, he would ask the company - or battalion - commander, 'What's the average age of your chaps?' Back would come the answer - twenty-three or thereabouts - and 'Monty' would remark, as if to himself, 'A good age... yes, a good age'.

At the Chilton Foliat inspection of the 506th, Montgomery continued the well-oiled procedure with the orders to the regimental commander, Colonel Sink, to tell his men to break ranks and rally around his jeep. Then he clambered on the bonnet of the little vehicle; he told them just how good they were, ending with the words that pleased the troopers no end, "After seeing the 506th, I pity the Germans!"

Two months later Churchill followed. As usual he was wearing his funny old-fashioned square bowler (derby) and smoking a big cigar. Military regulations didn't apply to Britain's prime minister. Together with his daughter, a second lieutenant in a mixed battery of the British Royal Artillery, he watched a mass jump, two battalions strong. Thereafter General Taylor asked the PM and the Supreme Commander, General Eisenhower, to inspect the troops. They obliged. 'Ike' stopped several times and posed the same old question he always did on such occasions. "Where are you from son?" Probably Eisenhower did not consciously hear the answer. It was part of the established routine -

32

the 'slapping of hands' that the Great American Public expected from its generals.

Churchill, for his part, must have hit upon an educated eagle in those tough, rough, airborne troopers. "Well son, how do you like England?" Churchill asked, and the trooper answered, "I like it very much", explaining that he had always enjoyed 'English literature and history'. The trooper recorded afterwards, 'It was a very memorable occasion'.

One man to whom Churchill spoke that day at Newbury would never tell the latter-day historians what the Great Man had said to him. He was General Don Pratt, the 101st's assistant commander. A superstitious man at the best of times, he would chide a fellow officer on 4th June for tossing his hat carelessly on his, Pratt's bed. He cried, "My God, that's bad luck!" Everyone present laughed, but Don Pratt wouldn't sit on that bed again... A mere forty-eight hours later he was dead, America's most senior officer to die on D-Day.

Now time was running out fast. But all was not well with the US Seventh Corps, commanded by General 'Lightning Joe' Collins. The youthful Irish-American general, who had gained his nickname and reputation in the Pacific would lead the assault on Utah Beach. Under his command would be the Fourth Infantry Division and the 101st AB. Both had been a very long time in training, yet some of their senior officers, especially those of the 4th, didn't really think they were one hundred per cent fitted for the ordeal to come.

In the event, their first practice exercise showed they weren't. They knew how to hit a beach, capture it and secure it against an enemy counter-attack. But at small unit level they seemed really not to know what to do next. Indeed they seemed to think that securing the initial position was sufficient (the 101st had more justification in thinking that this was what it was supposed to do). In fact, this was just the beginning.

Two short months before the actual assault, the 101st joined the rest of Collins' Seventh Corps in 'Exercise Beaver', the first practice run for D-Day itself. The site of the exercise was to be Slapton Sands, where surprisingly enough before the war, Montgomery himself had put a brigade ashore *in rowing boats!* Things were all high tech now. Too high tech many thought! For as the Fourth Division, 'The Ivy League', landed from the sea, followed by the seaborne elements of the 101st, the 'Screaming Eagles' glider and parachute infantry moved to their 'drop zones' in trucks. This was their simulated landing. The result was mass confusion!

The transit camps for the troops were ill-prepared. They didn't manage to feed and forward the 'Screaming Eagles' in time. The schedules went out of the window. The marshalling areas were little better. There were accidents, failure to arrive on time, soldiers, whole platoons of them, getting lost due to the fact that all signs had been long removed from the winding Devon roads and the MPs, who carried out the job of sign-posting in combat, hadn't done their tasks thoroughly enough. In the coarse phrase of the time, it was not just a 'SNAFU' but a real 'FUPBAR'.[9]

But according to the official historians of the time, 'valuable lessons were learned'. Well, if they were, the lessons were never completely absorbed by the time of D-Day, which was approaching even more rapidly. Once more the 101st would return to Slapton Sands, that then obscure part of the Devon coast, but which would, once the terrible secret was revealed (and it would take nearly forty years before it was) become infamous in the history of the events leading up to 6th June 1944. For at Slapton Sands ten times more GIs would be killed practising for the landings at Utah Beach in a single day than in the actual assault landing itself.

Throughout the last week of March '44, a series of conferences took place between the representatives of the 4th Infantry, the 101st Airborne and the US Navy. On 2nd April, an all-day 'critique' was conducted at Hamoaze House, in nearby Davenport in order to iron out these problems in time for the next exercise scheduled for 23-30th April. This was to be the biggest exercise yet and would go down in history as 'Operation Tiger'. Unfortunately soon someone else would have the tiger by the tail, namely the Germans!

On 25th April, the 'Screaming Eagles' got into position for their part in the last great exercise. Some of them were lodged in the swank surroundings of Torquay, including the famed 'Palm Court', used by wealthy British honeymoon couples before the war. It was vastly different to the real thing. The next day was closer to reality. The troops were shipped out to their assembly areas in trucks and most of them slept the next night in the fields till midnight. Then they were rudely awakened and taken to their simulated DZs. From here they marched, in the case of the 506th PIR, to an elevated position, from which through the morning mist they could view Slapton Beach below.

We could see a vast fleet of amphibious craft moving slowly into land. I've never seen so many ships together at one time, an invasion fleet is the most impressive sight in the whole world.

D. WEBSTER, 506TH PIR

What Webster didn't see that day, though he did note that the 'doughs' of the 4th Infantry Division coming through their lines were 'sweating, cursing and panting', was the overwhelming disaster which had taken place out at sea the previous evening.

Seven German S-Boats from Cherbourg had struck the convoy carrying the Fourth Division men at one minute after midnight. Their 'hits' were successful right from the start, but they seemed not to be too successful in sinking the Allied ships. Oberleutnant zur See Goetschke on the *S-140* soon reasoned why. The enemy were shallow-draft vessels: tank-landing aircraft and troop transports. Swiftly he and the rest turned over to firing their 4 cm cannon at the confused Americans. The slaughter had commenced ...

In the end a total of six hundred and thirty-nine men were reported killed or missing, including at least eight 'Bigots', that is officers who knew the top-secret details of D-Day, and perhaps another two hundred and fifty wounded. Immediately a news blackout was slapped on the disaster and details of the abortive operation were kept secret for years. Even today there are rumours that there are still secret mass graves in the general area of Slapton. The last great training exercise for the assault on Utah Beach had been a total and costly failure.

But the 'Screaming Eagles' were not allowed to know that - for obvious reasons. All the same some of them guessed that something had gone badly wrong. But what were they to do about it? Their mail home was censored anyway. Webster, who had been so impressed by the invasion fleet the day after the disaster, recalled that he and the rest of his company were warned by their officers that 'we cannot write about our Torquay excursion'. And that was that. Besides the 'Screaming Eagles' soon experienced a minor disaster of their own. On 9th May, the whole 101st Division was dropped on the Berkshire Downs round Hungerford and Newbury in a full-scale actual airborne rehearsal for D-Day. The jump was officially assessed as being 'seventy-five per cent accurate'. But twenty-eight Dakotas returned to base without dropping their troopers and there were four hundred and thirty-six casualties. Now there were exactly twenty-eight days left till D-Day. The future was obscure. What lay ahead for America's 'Screaming Eagles'? But if thirteen thousand odd of America's finest youth sensed some trepidation, they always felt confident they could carry out the task allotted to them. They had trained for two years for this task. They'd manage it - they had to. After all they were the 'Screaming Eagles'. As some of them cried exuberantly as they boarded their transports that day, *'Look out Hitler, here we come'*.

35

III

NORMANDY

On 5th June, Eisenhower had postponed D-Day for another twenty-four hours due to bad weather. Now on Tuesday 6th, it was on, bad weather or not. Eisenhower was still plagued by doubts. In particular he was concerned with the 101st Airborne, the 'Screaming Eagles', which British Air Marshal Leigh-Mallory had predicted would suffer eighty per cent casualties.

Our landings in the Cherbourg-Le Havre area have failed to gain a satisfactory foothold and I have withdrawn the troops. My decision to attack at this time and place was based upon the best information available. The troops, the air and the navy did all that bravery and devotion to duty could do. If any blame or fault attaches to the attempt, it is mine alone.

THE EISENHOWER MESSAGE NEVER SENT, MONDAY 5TH JUNE 1944

But although he had decided to go ahead with the invasion, 'Ike' was still worried. On the spur of the moment, he decided to visit the 'Screaming Eagles', the airborne division, which, if the British air marshal was to be believed, was doomed to be virtually wiped out on the other side of the Channel in a matter of hours. The journey was 'nightmarish'. The staff car fought D-Day traffic heading south to the camps along the coast all the way. Finally Eisenhower accompanied by his British aide, Brigadier Gault of the Guards, reached the airfield at Newbury.

A short time later we hard some noise and we went into the street between the tents to see what was going on. Down the street came the General, surrounded by his staff and a large number of photographers... Suddenly he came directly towards me and stopped. He asked my name and which State I came from. I gave him my name and told him I came from Michigan. He said, "Oh yes, Michigan... great fishing there... been there several times and like it". He then asked if I felt we were ready for the operation, did I feel we had been well briefed and were we all ready for the drop. I replied we were all set and didn't think it would have been too much of a problem. He seemed in good spirits. He chatted a little more which I believe was intended to relax us. I think that all of us being keyed up and ready to go buoyed *him* up somewhat... While I think the General thought his visit would boost the morale of our men, I honestly think it was *his* morale that was improved by such a remarkable 'high' group of troops.

WALLACE STROBEL, 502ND PARACHUTE INF.

The 'Screaming Eagles' were indeed in good heart and full of fight.

A little later as Eisenhower passed through the ranks of the black-faced paras, he met yet another who must have cheered him up. When 'Ike' asked him where he came from the kid replied, "Texas, sir..." He added, "Don't worry, sir, the 101st is on the job and everything will be taken care of in fine shape".

After the 'roll of honour', as Eisenhower's driver (some said mistress) British green-eyed, former model, Kay Summersby called it, General Eisenhower walked over to where General Maxwell Taylor was waiting. He accompanied the black-faced Taylor, the divisional commander, to his C-47 transport. Here they shook hands and Eisenhower knew that there was no more he could do. He walked slowly to the headquarters building and climbed to the roof. Here he watched as the transports rolled down the runway, plane after plane, to circle the field until whole flights came together in their final formations. At about midnight on 5th/6th June 1944, they had all gone.

"Well", Ike said to no one in particular, "it's on". He looked for another minute or so at the empty sky. Then he said, again to no one in particular, "No one can stop us now".

EISENHOWER'S DRIVER ON TUESDAY 6TH JUNE 1944

All went well till they reached the German-occupied Channel Islands, the only part of the British Isles to be taken by the enemy in World War Two. Here the 'Screaming Eagles' air armada hit trouble for the first time. Flak streamed up at the planes like a lethal Morse. Now as they approached the drop zone, the anti-aircraft fire intensified even more. 'It was like jumping into a Roman Candle', Lt. Col. Patrick Cassidy, C.O. of the 1st Battalion, 502nd Parachute Infantry Regiment, told himself. The flak unsettled some of the transport pilots under fire for the first time. They forgot their orders and their training. As they approached the green lights laid by the 'Screaming Eagles' pathfinders to indicate the 101st's drop zones, they were supposed to slow down before turning in towards the signal lamps. But the flak zipping towards them - blue, green, red - unnerved them. Instead of slowing down, they increased speed. Their first thought now was to escape from this terrifying sight of sudden death and destruction.

Here they were thrust into the very jaws of this violence and they had never had one minute of combat experience, so that they were absolutely terrified. And rather than throttle down, they were kind of like the fellow thinking with his feet; they thought with that throttle... They said, 'My God, commonsense will tell me the quicker I get out of here, the better chance I have of surviving, and that's unfortunate for the boys back there, but be

that as it may, I'm getting out of here.'
GORDON CARSON, 506TH PARACHUTE INFANTRY

Fortunately, however, for the success of the airborne drop that Tuesday morning, most of the pilots, as inexperienced in combat as they were, pressed on to start dropping the 101st. They dropped low. They lost their equipment. They jumped from blazing planes. They sprang out from transports that were miles off target. But they jumped.

In essence, their objective was to secure the exits from the infantry landing sites at Utah Beach. The beach itself was a gently rising series of low sand dunes, with few houses for the defenders to dig in or cliffs such as those at Omaha, where the terrible slaughter depicted in *Private Ryan* took place. The problem was the farming roads leading inland from Utah Beach. They were elevated above the fields, which were now flooded on Field Marshal Rommel's orders, thus forcing artillery and armour to use them, becoming an easy target for the German bunkers and artillery emplacements located in the area beyond the flooded fields.

These 'causeways', as Eisenhower called them, had to be captured and the guns beyond seized by a speedy 'coup de main' before the Germans had time to rally after the surprise airdrop. This was the 'Screaming Eagles' task. Speed and precision were of the essence.

This General Maxwell Taylor knew. The veteran of the previous year's Sicily landing knew too that airborne operations were always chaotic. They never went as planned. Good commanders had to be prepared for losses, even large ones. Good commanders would have to rally as many men as they could speedily round up and go hell-for-leather for their objectives before the Germans had time to recover. This he had instilled into his regimental and battalion commanders time and time again. He hoped now, as he hit the deck, that they would do so.

Taylor, who had jumped only a couple of times before, landed to find himself in a worse position than any of his commanders. He was totally alone - and lost.

I landed alone in a field surrounded by the usual high hedges and trees with a few cows as witnesses. The rest of my stick went into an adjacent field... The area into which I wandered was covered with field fortifications, newly-constructed, but fortunately I encountered no Germans.
GEN. MAXWELL TAYLOR

41

For twenty minutes the General wandered around by himself until he bumped into a Private of the 501st Parachute Infantry. The latter was surprised out of his wits when he discovered he was being given a great big bear-hug not by a German, but by his commanding officer.

One by one, General Taylor and the lone Private collected more and more men. Unfortunately most of them seemed to be staff officers with only a few riflemen - the 'poor bloody infantry' - who did the actual fighting. These would be soon needed for the little group of airborne troopers were slowly approaching German-held Poupeville. By nine that Tuesday morning the 'brass-heavy group' was in position to attack. In the end Taylor had to order in the only fighting troops he could find, men of Colonel Ewell's Third Battalion, 501st Parachute Infantry. Two hours of nerve-racking house-to-house fighting followed. But with the aid of the staff, the place was finally captured and the 101st's divisional staff was able to take over the German Headquarters in the little town. The first of the Utah Beach exits was almost in American hands.

Never in the history of military operations have so few been commanded by so many.

GEN. TAYLOR, EVENING 6TH JUNE 1944

But now the Germans were really beginning to react. The 101st were taking casualties. Here and there they were even being forced out of the positions they had captured before dawn. One reason was that they lacked heavy weapons to tackle German armour and mobile artillery; for the initial artillery support the 'Screaming Eagles' had reckoned with had failed to appear. The Division's 377th Parachute Field Artillery Battalion had been parachuted into flooded fields, marshes and swamps, where they had lost all but one of their 75 mm howitzers. General Maxwell Taylor needed 'bodies' urgently. The time had come for General Don Pratt's glider-borne infantry to land ...

Generals, on the whole, are prima donnas. Perhaps, with their job, they have to be. American airborne generals, who led tough, often ill-disciplined paratroopers, seemed to have been cast very much in that mould. General Taylor had two such junior generals under command: Brigadier-General 'Tony' McAuliffe, his artillery commander, and General Pratt, in charge of his three thousand strong glider-borne battalions.

For instance, on the very same 4th June, when Pratt refused to sleep on his bed because it was 'unlucky' due to the unknown officer throwing his cap upon it, McAuliffe got pretty high in the officers'

42

club. The 'Crock', as McAuliffe was known, staggered back to his quarters and promptly shot up his room with his beloved tommy-gun. Other officers tried to reason with the future hero of 'the siege' of Bastogne, the 101st's most celebrated engagement in World War Two. To no avail. In the end General Taylor personally had to disarm the tough old 'Crock' and forbid him to carry the sub-machine gun with him into battle on D-Day.

Pratt was no McAuliffe. But he was jealous of the prestige of his glider-borne troops, who weren't volunteers like the paratroopers of the 101st, but drafted men. He insisted they ranked as highly as the men who jumped out of aeroplanes. After all, his glider troops went to battle in flimsy canvas and wooden planes lacking an engine; they were also very dangerous, as casualties were to prove. And naturally General Pratt was very concerned with his own standing and the trappings of his rank.

This was exemplified by the glider in which he would lead his men into battle. It was marked with a very large 'No. 1' and General Pratt would sit next to the pilot of the glider in the co-pilot's seat. In effect, if all went well, General Pratt would be the first fighting glider soldier to land on French soil. Today, it is not known whether the General or his staff was behind the 'customising' Glider No. 1 to make it as safe as possible for Pratt. But it was 'customised' in a manner that made the Waco glider a death trap for the General.

Usually pilots in the flimsy gliders sat on their flimsy flak jackets. They weren't going to chance losing the 'family jewels' to a lucky shot from below. In the case of the General, his seat was armour-plated with additional protection being added at the very last moment, so that no time was available to test the influence of this extra weight on the overall trim of 'Glider No. 1'.

The result was predictable. General Pratt's glider came in first, hissing at tree-top height at well over a hundred miles an hour. It slammed to the ground in a cloud of dust. It skidded forward, spun out of control, due to the extra weight, smashed into a hedgerow and came to an abrupt stop.

The pilot had both legs broken. But the General didn't move. He was dead. The extra weight had crushed him to death. Later it was given out he died instantly. I wonder.

MAJOR V. WARRINER, GLIDER PILOT, USAAF

General Pratt was unlucky. Perhaps he had been right that afternoon two days before when he had blown his top at the officer who had thrown down his cap on his bunk. Or perhaps he had sensed that his luck had run out.

It had, too, for many of the other gliders that followed General Pratt to his death, the first US general to be killed in action on the Continent in World War Two. But now the casualties were limited, though most of the gliders were badly damaged or complete write-offs. That didn't matter. There were plenty of new gliders available. What was important that June day was that the glider infantry's weapons and supplies remained intact - jeeps, anti-tank guns, rations and medical stores - even a small bulldozer! This has been intended for the 101st's 326th Airborne Engineers. But they were so scattered to do much good - or need a bulldozer - just then.

Still the addition of three thousand odd men was just what a hard-pressed General Taylor needed. Two exits (causeways) had been secured by now and at four o'clock that afternoon, a grimy, battle-worn GI of the 101st met the first equally worn infantry men from the 4th Infantry Division coming up from Utah Beach with, 'Where the hell have you guys been?' The infantryman's reply is not recorded, but one doesn't need a crystal ball to guess what it could have been.

With the two forces, the 101st and the 4th Infantry, linked up, however tenuously, the 'Screaming Eagles' could start evacuating their casualties down to the Utah Beach. There were plenty of them, but by now the paratroopers had captured a few German trucks to carry their wounded back to the sands. In charge they had a few lightly wounded men, guarding numerous German prisoners-of-war who were used to doing the fetching and carrying. They included two who had spent the day hidden in the Screaming Eagles' command post. The Frenchwoman who had hidden them there told Colonel Cassidy of the First Battalion, 502nd Parachute Infantry, that they had been 'very kind to me' during their stay on the Invasion Front. Cassidy reserved his comment, but he could guess what form their kindness had taken. The French landlady looked a very happy woman!

At the same time as the wounded were sent to the rear, Cassidy's radio man reached the divisional CP of the 4th Infantry on the beach. There he encountered General 'Tubby' Barton, commander of the 'Ivy League Division', as it was known on account of its divisional patch. He told the General that 'the enemy gun positions near St. Martin' had been captured.

"That's the best news I've had in many hours," Barton, who would be the first US General to cross into Germany, but lose his division almost twice over in the process, replied, "Now what about the causeways?"

The radioman didn't know. But he returned to Cassidy's command post, and was able to report back that the causeway west of St. Martin had seemingly been cleared of the enemy, 'Exit No. 4 is now open and ready for your advance'.

But the battle to clear the causeways was not over yet. Brave men were still to die clearing them for the Fourth and cowards would skulk and leave the fighting to those who would take the initiative that might well sign their death warrant.[10]

One such brave man was Staff Sergeant Harrison Summers of the 502nd. He picked up a group and advanced into the unknown. He tackled a barracks complex on the Reuville road. He charged and killed four Germans with his tommy-gun. He cleared a second barracks by the same method. Behind him his men set up a light machine gun and took the third barracks under fire. Now totally alone, Summers darted forward, kicked down a door in the third small barracks and killed six Germans with a long deadly burst from his Thompson. The rest of the Germans surrendered and there was the deafened, begrimed sergeant surrounded by Germans with no one to deal with them.

It was at that juncture that a Private John Camden wandered, slightly puzzled, into the action. He asked the NCO: "Why are we doing this?" He meant tackling the Germans single-handed; sooner or later the lone warrior was going to get killed.

Summers shrugged, "I don't know," he said. "What about the others?" Again Summers looked puzzled. "They don't seem to want to fight and I can't make them. So I've got to finish it."

PRIVATE CAMIEN, 502ND PARACHUTE INFANTRY REGIMENT

Thereupon Camien joined the brave sergeant. A few of the others did the same. They cleared five houses, leaving a trail of thirty dead Germans behind them. They came across a bunch of Germans, unsuspectingly eating their breakfast. They didn't live to finish it. Not a German was spared. In the end the rest of the Germans fled and were later picked up by the doughboys of the 4th Infantry. Sergeant Summers was rewarded with a battlefield commission.

For most of that day, I felt alone on the Cotentin (peninsula).

GEN. MAXWELL TAYLOR

The situation was little better on the German side. Their senior commanders were away at conference at Rennes. Hammered by incessant low-level allied fighter-bomber attacks, they were finding it very difficult to return to take over their duties. One who did, the general commanding the German 91st Division, a formation which had been specifically trained in anti-airborne operations, was killed by such a Jabo[11], as the Germans called the feared fighter-bombers.

One low-level, but important ground commander, Major von der Heydte, C.O. of the elite 6th German Parachute Regiment, was naturally well versed in anti-airborne operations. Normally he would have known exactly what should be done. But the aristocratic Catholic commander, with the face of a medieval knight, seemed strangely lethargic this June day.

> The sun was shining [and the whole scene] reminded me of a summer's day on the Wannsee.
>
> MAJOR VON DER HEYDTE

Perhaps it was the fact that, due to the scattered drop, the whole 'Ami' (as the Germans called the Americans) attack seemed difficult to pinpoint. Although von der Heydte had viewed the actual D-Day armada from the church steeple of St-Come-du-Mont, he still didn't know where exactly to send his three battalions into the counter-attack.

When he did, the German paratroop veteran of Crete, Africa and Russia, lost contact with his men almost immediately. The result was that one of his battalions, engaged by the waiting 'Screaming Eagles' of the 501st Parachute Regiment at the La Barquette lock area, began to crack almost at once. Perhaps the best-trained soldiers of the whole anti-Invasion force who had sworn a personal oath, not only to the Führer as was customary, but to the German Parachute Regiment, lost their will to fight. They started to surrender in droves. In the end, three hundred and fifty of them had given up to the 101st troopers.

> You are the elite of the German Army...
> Your greatest ambition should be to do battle...
> Never surrender.
> For you it is either victory or death; there is no other alternative.
> This is a point of honour.
>
> THE TEN COMMANDMENTS OF THE SIXTH GERMAN PARACHUTE REGIMENT

Rapidly the Catholic aristocrat, von der Heydte, was becoming disillusioned by the way he was being attacked and at the same time being ordered by the High Command to hold his positions against what now appeared to be three 'Ami' divisions. 'Hold, hold! Defend to the last man... that's all we heard from Hitler', the Baron complained bitterly after the war. 'It was impossible.'

Throughout the 7th and 8th June, his Sixth continued to attack in an attempt to dislodge the airborne troops of both the 101st and their sister division, 'the All Americans' of the US 82nd Airborne. In vain. And all the time his casualties were mounting dramatically. Thus it was that by Friday 9th June 1944, the Baron had decided he couldn't sacrifice his precious regiment needlessly. Secretly he started to withdraw his men from the line in the St Mere-Eglise area. As he explained later, 'I found a way. I established an aid post for the wounded a safe distance behind the lines and every day I sent men back, wounded or not'.

The time was right. Already his First Battalion had pulled back from their battle with the airborne troopers to his headquarters - *twenty-five men* left of the original seven hundred!

That same time as enemy guns from the 4th Division pounded his positions, an American officer appeared in front of von der Heydte's HQ bearing a looted French tablecloth on a broom pole. The 'Ami' explained he had a message from General Maxwell Taylor. It was written in German and demanded the 6th Parachute Regiment should surrender immediately. The Baron, who had been a Carnegie Scholar in the States and was proud of his English, replied in that language stating that he couldn't comply and asked Taylor: "What would you do in my place?"

Later that day, the Baron was informed by his corps headquarters that they had supplies for his trapped regiment, but that didn't matter; 'Parachutists only need knives'. But HQ did relent. They smuggled through a shipment of mortar bombs but the disgusted Baron found they were of French manufacture[12] and didn't fit his mortars. But his resourceful Fallschirmjager wrapped the shells in blankets so that they fitted the tubes and fired the French shells that way. One item of re-supply, however, was the final straw as far as the Baron was concerned. It was dropped by air and his paras risked their lives to crawl out and retrieve the large pack. To their disgust, it was found to contain what the German soldiers called 'Parisians', i.e. contraceptives!

What does Corps HQ expect us to do - fuck our way out!
BARON VON DER HEYDTE, JUNE 1944

On that same Friday, while the 82nd AB and 4th Infantry were preparing to support the newly arrived 90th Infantry Division in his (as it turned out) abortive attempt to finally break out of the beach head in the drive for the key port of Cherbourg, the 101st was still struggling to organise and achieve its original objectives.

The 101st had been dropped over scores of miles and there were still some two thousand paratroopers of the original drop missing. In essence the 'Screaming Eagles' were still fighting small unit actions, in which handfuls of brave and desperate men attempted to capture features that had been originally allotted to whole battalions and companies. It was the time of the brave, the individualist, the unconventional.

Screaming Eagle, Private Burgett, came across one such para. He spotted a group and joined in, heading for, as far as he was concerned, the unknown. A tall trooper took over the motley group. For some reason he ordered his 'command' to double-time. They did so seemingly automatically, until they came to other 'Screaming Eagles', lying in ditches and doorways firing in the direction of Ste Marie du Mont. One of the men in the firing line shouted that Ste Marie had not been taken yet.

The tall troopers yelled back, "Hell, we know that. But we've got other things to do right now". And so they jogged on, ignoring the slugs cutting the air all around.

Others of the 'Screaming Eagles' went on a mission of their own. In *War and Peace* Tolstoy wrote war was an excuse for common soldiers to wander around. This 19th century Russian writer was right. Soldiers do wander around battlefields, looking for loot, souvenirs, even women. But mostly they do so on foot and in a non-flamboyant manner.

Not so the unknown airborne trooper of the 101st on that Friday. He was seen riding a looted white horse, with twin Lugers strapped around his waist, charging towards a German machine gun post, yelling in time-honoured *Lone Ranger* fashion, 'Hi Ho Silver!' This time, however, the 'masked avenger' didn't pull it off. On his third attempt at charging the Germans, they fired a burst at close range. His body, cut almost in half, was flung out of the saddle - and this time there was no Tonto to save the unfortunate trooper...

One day later, with the survivors of the great jump now consolidating their position into a firm line, the dead General Pratt's glidermen were sent to attack Carentan and link up with the US 29th Division, which had landed with the 1st Division at Omaha. But the city was held in strength and 327th Regiment was stopped dead by the enemy after advancing six hundred yards. Now the Third Battalion of the 502nd Parachute Infantry was thrown in to get the attack moving once more. But the opposition was tough.

Carentan was surrounded by marshes and the usual network of causeway roads, which channelled traffic and men into the funnels that were dominated by German 88s and machine gun nests. It was an ideal place for a handful of determined men to hold off whole regiments. And that was what the German High Command intended. For finally they realised that the Utah landings were not just a feint as the Führer had predicted. This was the real thing. However, Rommel and his subordinate commanders had not reckoned with Taylor's 'Screaming Eagles'.

The paratroopers attacked under the command of their C.O., Colonel Cole. They fought their way to the 'island' on which the city of Carentan was built. But here the steam went out of their attack. The men started to go to ground. Colonel Cole, knowing the importance of their attack, wasn't going to have that. He looked around at the red-faced, sweating paras sharing a ditch with him and yelled above the angry snap-and-crack of the small arms battle, "Everybody fix bayonets... reload rifles with a full clip". Obediently his men started to carry out the C.O.'s orders, already aware of what was to come. "Be ready to move out at the sound of the whistle", Cole continued a moment or two later.

He waited. The men were finally ready, though some appeared definitely reluctant to go 'over the top', as they had called it in the old war. Cole stood up in full view of the enemy. He shrilled a blast on his whistle. Without waiting to see if his men were following him, Colonel Cole clambered over the edge of the ditch. At a quick pace, he started to stumble across the shell-pocked field towards the enemy positions and the waiting machine guns. Some followed. Others hesitated. A few pretended they hadn't heard the whistle. At least that's what they said afterwards.

His lack of numbers didn't seem to worry the brave Colonel. Carried away by the wild unreasoning blood lust of battle, he headed straight for the Germans. The faltered at the sight of the paras armed with bayonets. Suddenly they broke. They started streaming back everywhere. Minutes later the main position was taken and once again a handful of brave Screaming Eagles had carried out a task intended for a whole battalion.

Thus it was that Colonel Cole won the 101st Airborne's first Medal of Honor, the highest award for bravery in action that the United States Congress could bestow on its soldiers. It wouldn't be the Division's last MOH by any means. But Colonel Cole would be one of the Division's recipients in World War Two to gain that high honour and live to tell the tale. The next one, Private Mann of Holland, would die in the arms of his comrades within minutes of winning the medal for outstanding bravery and self-sacrifice. That long-forgotten private soldier of over half a century ago would be one of the long line of 'Screaming Eagles' who have won the award in the years to come in every battle that the USA has fought since that fateful year of 1944. Most of them were soon forgotten by their 'grateful' country.

IV

HOLLAND

Back in August 1942 when the 101st Airborne had been first formed at Camp Claiborne in the USA, Major General Lee (as the 'Father of the US Airborne' would soon be) told his fledging paratroopers: '[you have] no history but... a rendezvous with destiny. Like the early American pioneers whose invincible courage was the foundation of this nation, we have broken with the past and its traditions in order to establish our claim to the future'.

They had been somewhat flamboyant words for Lee, who was not given to such rhetoric normally, but they had proved true. The 'Screaming Eagles', which he had trained and of which he had been so proud, had had their 'rendezvous with destiny' in Normandy and had met its challenge bravely and successfully. But the price of the 101st had had to pay had been high. Indeed the butcher's bill had been exceedingly costly and in Washington, here and there, voices were raised again to question whether airborne divisions could be justified in the light of such high losses.

Of the 6,600 men of the 101st who had dropped on that Tuesday morning in June, some 3,500 were listed as missing by midnight that same night. By the time the whole of the Division had returned to its English bases in mid-July, some eight hundred and sixty-eight men were posted as killed in action, nearly two thousand as wounded and hundreds were already in the Reich behind the wire of German POW cages. When, for instance, Sergeant Ed Hughes of the Division's 501st Parachute Infantry returned to the 101st after recovering from his wound, he waited to meet a bus containing the survivors of his 2nd Platoon. Exactly twelve men got off. He asked in surprise, "Where's the rest?" The answer was grim and sombre: "This is it. There are no more".

The old division which the soon-to-die General Lee had created had vanished. Now the time had come to create another one. It was tough going. Some four thousand replacements had to be absorbed, some to make up for the men who were allowed to transfer out; they had had enough of the dangers of 'going airborne'. But the nucleus of the old division still was intact. Unlike their old rivals of the 6th British Airborne Division who had dropped on the other flank of the D-Day Invasion, they hadn't lost so many of their battalion and company commanders which had followed in the British sector after the initial landing. These 'old heads', officers and non-coms, soon started to work, knocking the 'new boys' into shape.

And speed was of the essence. As July 1944 gave way to August, with the Allies now breaking out of their beachheads in France, airborne missions came pouring in to the 'Screaming Eagles' HQ. Within the space of some six weeks or so, *twelve* specific airborne operations were proposed, which had the staff working all out to prepare the details of the air assault. Indeed one mission got so far that the 'Screaming Eagles' were actually assembled in full combat gear on their fields ready for take-off before the operation was cancelled. Later General Maxwell Taylor, who was becoming ever more unpopular among the rank-and-file as a 'glory hunter', assembled the whole division and apologised for the cancellation of the mission. The result was that he was roundly booed by the troops!

> I could never understand anyone as obviously brilliant as Maxwell Taylor. How could he overlook the enlisted man's point of view as far as to assume that every private, non-com and junior officer there was just as anxious to return to combat as he, a West Point general, was.
>
> J. MASURA, 101ST AB

But as September that year came, with victory in the air, the pundits and armchair warriors in Washington predicting the war would be over by Christmas, the 'Screaming Eagles' finally received a definite combat mission, whether they liked it or not.

It was the famous or infamous (depending upon which way one looks at it) 'Operation Market Garden',[13] planned by the newly knighted 'Sir' Bernard Law Montgomery, or the 'Limey fart', as General George Patton was wont to call him. By now the US Army had arrived at the Siegfried Line, the Third Reich's last man-made defensive line. But already the American Generals were finding it tough going and, in due course, they'd find it even tougher. General Patton, Commander of the US Third Army, would boast that if he was given sufficient supplies of fuel, ammunition and men, he'd go through the Siegfried Line 'like crap through a goose'. He'd be maintaining the same statement four months later when he was still battering his head at the fortification that ran from Southern Holland right to the Swiss border. Montgomery planned to circumvent Hitler's 'Westwall' by outflanking it.

It was a daring plan. At the beginning no one thought it was too daring, though there were objections raised within the British camp at field officer level. But as far as the US top brass, who would castigate Monty's plan *afterwards* were concerned, there seemed no hesitation in going along with it at the time. In that September General Bradley, the American Army Group Commander, could say to Patton, 'It is one of the most imaginative [plans] of the year'. Later he wasn't so complimentary.

> Had the pious tee-totalling Montgomery wobbled into SHAEF with a hangover, I could not have been more astonished than I was by the daring operation he proposed!
>
> GEN. BRADLEY, 1948

In essence, Market Garden envisaged the Allied Airborne Army to jump at specific points along a fifty-mile long highway from the British Front in Belgium to Arnhem deep in Holland. The three Allied airborne divisions involved would capture key bridges along this route to ensure that the British XXX Corps could link up with the paras of the British 1st AB Division at Arnhem. Thereafter the Allies would race from Arnhem across the nearby border into the Reich and from there head for the German capital, Berlin. In the case of the 'Screaming Eagles', they would drop closest to the link-up force from the British XXX Corps: the Guards Armoured Division, whose divisional patch was an eye. (Wags cracked that the eye winked whenever it spotted a virgin, but it never winked once in the whole course of the war in Europe). The 101st would land between Son (sometimes known as 'Zon') and St Oedenrode and also in Veghel. Here they would capture the key bridges, so that the Guards could drive on through the positions of the US 82nd AB and then onwards to Arnhem. Determination and speed were going to be vital, if the lightly armed 1st Airborne, 'The Red Devils', were going to hold their bridge across the Rhine. The time scale for the whole daring operation to be completed was between forty-eight an ninety-six hours. In the event, some of the 'Screaming Eagles' would still be fighting in the area as late as November 1944...

Sunday 17th September 1944. The weather was warm and sunny. Over the DZs the forecast was excellent: clear and light winds, ideal for a para-drop. Those who had a few moments to read the English Sunday papers had been informed by the London scandal sheet, *The News of the World*, that Hitler's batman had been captured the previous day in Belgium. A likely tale! He had informed his interrogators that his former boss 'alternated between kindness and brutality and is very nervous... He is not averse to blondes. One of them is a typist who visits him in a fast car'. Now the blonde in the fast car was forgotten as below crowds of people came out on the street to wave at the departing aerial armada. There was even a Salvation Army band, leaving the local 'Citadel', who struck up a rousing march when they saw the Dakotas heading east.

Crowds continued to cheer the 'Screaming Eagles' and their comrades of the 82nd and 1st British AB divisions. But as soon as their transports and the tugs towing the gliders crossed the British XXX Corps' front line on the Belgian-Dutch border, the cheering ceased.

Instead of hand waving, German gun-layers started pulling their firing handles. Tracer, red, white and green, began zipping upwards dangerously, frighteningly.

Worse was to come, once the 'Eagles' began to jump. For a little while they were sitting ducks. The Germans tackled them with rifle and machine gun fire, and in some cases with their feared quadruple flak, which the airborne troopers rightly called 'meat-choppers'. They did rip the helpless men drifting down slowly to bloody pieces. Some of the men who had dropped in Normandy had anticipated this sort of reception and had come prepared. They had undone the safety clip of their chutes and a few had even turned the release clip and pulled upon the bellyband - with fatal consequences. They fell out of their chutes as the wind billowed out the canopies and pulled the parachute from their bodies.

Well one of the guys... he came out of the chute... He hit the thatched roof of a haystack, ricocheted and hit the ground. You could see his arms and legs wind- milling and they kept getting smaller. All his bones were breaking.

DON BUGGETT, 506 PI RGT.

Once the survivors had landed, the action seemed to get even more bitter. The Germans were everywhere; mixed bunches of ordinary 'Landsers', Air Force men and a few elite German paratroopers, commanded by General Student, the victor of Rotterdam and Crete, whose airborne 'coups de main' had been the model for 101st's original instructors back in 40/41.

Still, despite the casualties, the confusion, the absolute chaos in some places, the 'Screaming Eagles' pressed home their attack, heading for the all-important bridges. Without them Horrocks XXX Corps limited, in essence, to one road, would never reach the 'Red Devils', how heading for the 'bridge too far' at Arnhem.

General Taylor was pleased, however, with progress so far. The 101st jump had been 'unusually successful - almost like an exercise'. Back in the UK he had anticipated casualties of at least thirty per cent. In fact most of the 6,669 paratroopers who had jumped had landed safely and although the gliders, as usual were having their problems, they were landing their cargoes of supplies and essential transport in the form of jeeps. Indeed General McAuliffe, who would come in soon, was fast asleep when his glider began its landing pattern!

Several live bullets ricocheted off the metal tubing, while others passed through the fabric with a loud pop... Now the general was wide-awake and wanted to know if there was some way to shoot back at 'those bastards'. He even suggested knocking in the entry door so that he could fire at them.

MAJOR WARRINER, TROOP CARRIER COMMAND

All the same, Taylor knew that he was fifteen miles ahead of the British Guards and he had to capture the key bridges so that they could roll north by nightfall. At lightning speed, his men took Veghel, the northern-most objective along that single road, known as the 'corridor'. With it, his 'Screaming Eagles' captured the four bridges across the River Aa and the Willems Canal. To the south, halfway between Son and Veghel, Taylor's paras captured the small, but important town of St. Oedenrode. With it the highway, that crossed over the Rommel River, fell into the Americans' hands too. It seemed that the 101st was having the easiest time of the three Allied airborne divisions, making the best use of the initial surprise which had caught the German defenders unaware.[14]

Unfortunately for the 'Screaming Eagles' and indeed the whole operation, the Allies' luck was beginning to run out. The Germans were now reacting with speed and determination, under the command of such tough leaders as General Student and Field Marshal Model, who both chanced to be in the area that day. Almost immediately their troops started to counter-attack the single main highway leading north to Arnhem. The result was that the drive of the Guards Armoured Division along the key road began to slow down. By mid-afternoon, a now worried Taylor knew that the Guards wouldn't be reaching their day's objective, Valkenswaard, to link up with the paras and enable the combined force to seize the other local targets.

Already Brigadier 'Joe' Vandeleur, leading the Irish Guards' Battle Group, which was to make the link-up with the 'Yanks', was running into serious trouble. The big, red-faced veteran tank commander hadn't liked the assignment right from the start. During the briefing by XXX Corps Commander, Brian Horrocks, he had reacted to the news of his assignment with 'Not us again, surely!' "What did you say?" Horrocks asked. In a flash the Brigadier replied: "I said how honoured we feel, sir". "Yes", said Horrocks, who had a fine sense of humour, remarking, "That's what I thought you said".

A Sherman manned by Sergeant Capewell fixed a whole magazine into a German armed with a panzerfaust. He threw up his arms and fell dead. But it didn't stop the enemy knocking out

Capewell's tank. Behind him Major M. O'Cock watched in horror as nine Shermans in front of him were systematically knocked out one by one. In a space of half a mile the whole lead element had been wrecked. Next to me on the factory roof, another staff officer groaned, 'My God, they won't get through'.

STAFF OFFICER ON GEN. HORROCKS' XXX CORPS STAFF

That afternoon the most important of Taylor's objectives - the highway ridge over the Wilhelmina Canal at Son, had still not been captured. It was located five miles north of the key town of Eindhoven, home of the great Phillips electrical firm. As a contingency plan, the General now decided to seize a bridge over the canal at Best, four miles to the west. As it was only a secondary bridge, the 'Screaming Eagles' commander sent a single company only to capture it. It was a bad mistake.

The Germans, under the command of General Student, whose HQ was only ten miles away, reacted in strength 'H' company, the one sent to attack, came under fire immediately and the battle which ensued and, which lasted over two further days, would finally involve a whole parachute regiment.

In the battle which followed, Colonel Cole, the Division's first Medal of Honour winner, was horrified to see his men being strafed by friendly planes. "Screw the bridge!" he yelled and dashed out to stop the air attack. This time he was out of luck. He was shot in the head and died instantly. He never did receive that medal from Eisenhower.

But in that same battle the second member of the 101st to win the coveted honour did so. He was Private Joe Mann. Already he had been wounded twice in his arms but had refused to be evacuated. Now Mann and his surviving companions came under a severe German hand grenade attack. The Germans showed no mercy on the trapped 'Amis'. A comrade had one eye blown out and the other was blinded by a grenade as he huddled next to Mann, whose both arms were now tightly bound up in slings. Now it was Mann's turn. A grenade landed in front of him. But burdened as he was, there was nothing he could do about the stick grenade.

"Grenade! I'm taking this one!" he yelled. He flung himself backwards on the grenade just as it exploded. A couple of the men were wounded. But Mann's sacrifice had saved their lives. "My back is gone", he said softly and then he died without a single moan.'

PTE SMITH, 101ST AIRBORNE

Private Mann had the sad honour of being the second member of the 101st AB Division to receive the Congressional Medal of Honor. But like the first recipient, he was dead too.

While H Company was being decimated in its attempt to capture the secondary bridge at Best, men of Colonel Sink's 506th Regiment were going for the main highway bridge at Son. At first they made good progress against no opposition. But as the advance party reached the outskirts of the village of Son all hell broke loose. Worse still, when the advancing 'Eagles' were within fifty yards of the bridge itself, there was a sudden throaty crunch. The bridge shook and began to vibrate alarmingly. The inevitable happened; the bridge went up. Still the men under Sink's command were not going to give up that easily. A three-man team under the leadership of Major James Le Prade dived into the canal and swam across. Other members of the battalion followed. Hastily they set up a bridgehead and then, with the help of patriotic Dutch civilians, they constructed a temporary bridge, using the old bridge's still intact trestle.

> The bridge was unsatisfactory from every point of view, except it did enable me to put back the rest of the regiment across in single file.
>
> COL. SINK

Now, for the time being, the 'corridor' at Son was reduced to a single wooden treadway across the canal ...

The fighting had now become savage, almost primeval, down to hand-to-hand combat where no quarter was given or expected. One of the 101st's 'new boys', Frank Whiting, for instance, was caught by surprise and captured. But Whiting grabbed for his captor's rifle. A bitter hand-to-hand battle commenced in freezing swamp water. Whiting choked his captor almost into unconsciousness, his fingers bitten through to the bone by the German. Suddenly he remembered his abandoned rifle. He grabbed it, slammed the butt against the German's chest. The enemy soldier fell, but like a boxer who refused to go down for the count, he tried to get up once more. Whiting choked and gasped. Blindly he fired a round into the German's back in the same instant that a Lt. Mosier ran up and asked, "Are you okay?"

Whiting couldn't speak. All he could do was to point to the prone figure opposite. Mosier didn't hesitate. He drew his knife and fell upon the German, driving his knife into him savagely. The German didn't get up again.

"Where are you going with that prisoner, Trooper?" General Taylor asked. The trooper pointed to the POW who was wearing US paratrooper combat boots and whose hands he had tied behind his back. "Gonna drown this little bastard in the canal, General". "I don't think we should do that, soldier." Gently he removed the German from the irate soldier's custody.

EUGENE 'RED' FLANAGAN

In some cases discipline broke down. The strain and stress of battle was too much for the hard-pressed airborne troopers. A battalion commander was observed to shoot two Germans through a window when they were sitting at a table. He could have easily taken them prisoner, but the blood rage of battle was too much. Indeed any German who was slow in putting up his hands when surrendering usually didn't live long. Snipers were shot out of hand, whether they wanted to surrender or not. Discipline tended to crumple too even when it was that between men of the same side. According to the stories of the time, airborne troopers were always threatening to do something drastic to the 'Limeys' when they appeared tardy. The British appeared to the Americans to be always stopping 'for tea'. What the Americans never realised was the strict water discipline of the British Army. American soldiers could drink whenever it suited them. British soldiers, trained for the water shortages of action in remoter and hotter spots of the British Empire, had to have an officer's permission before taking a drink from their water-bottle or taking time off for their much needed 'brew-up'.[15]

Within the ranks of the 101st itself there were repeated cases of insubordination as the fighting grew ever more bitter and intense. One of the most dramatic and poignant of these became a central part in the Hollywood epic *The Bridge Too Far*. It concerned the true story of Sergeant Charles Dohun, who went looking for his company commander near Best. The Sergeant's C.O., Captain LeGrand Johnson, had been left in the 'dead pile'. Apparently he had been killed by a shot through the head and left shoulder. Dohun wasn't satisfied. He had promised Johnson he would never die. Carried away by a kind of mad grief, he burst into an aid tent where an M.O. was working frantically on a never-ending stream of wounded paras. "Major", he said, "my captain needs attention right away".

"I'm sorry, Sergeant", the surgeon replied. "We'll get to him. He'll have to wait."

The NCO wouldn't leave. The M.O. raised his head once again from the bloody wreck of a man he was working on and added threateningly, as if he was about to pull rank, "Sergeant, we've got a lot of wounded men here. Your captain will be attended to as soon as we get to him".

That did it. Dohun drew his big .45 automatic from its leather holster. He pulled back the receiver slowly and cocked it. With both hands, as cops do now in modern Hollywood movies, he aimed the weapon directly at the startled M.O.'s face. "It's not soon enough", he said through gritted teeth. "Major, I'll kill you right where you stand if you don't look at him right away."

The Major gave in. He commanded the orderlies to bring in Captain Johnson. While a grim-faced Dohun watched, the medic went straight to work on the possibly dead para captain. He was operated upon and then received a massive blood transfusion. The colour returned to his cheeks and a weary Major looked up finally and told Dohun that his C.O. would survive. He'd wake up with 'one hell of a headache', but he'd live.

It was then that Dohun surrendered his weapon and waited for the inevitable. The angry doctor sent for the MPs. They arrested Dohun and took him to his battalion command post. Here his battalion commander, Lt. Col. Chappuis, heard Dohun's tale and said, "I'm placing you under arrest for exactly one minute". Together the men stood there facing each other, wrapped up in their own thoughts. Finally Chappuis looked at his wristwatch. "All right", he snapped. "The minute's up. Dismissed. Now get back to your unit." And that was that.

Nearly half a century later, Hollywood actor James Caan, would play that scene in *The Bridge Too Far* movie to perfection ...

But at the time, the dramatic episode would soon be forgotten. There were too many of them and the 101st and their allies of the Guards Armoured Division, who had now arrived, were fighting for their very lives.

Jim, never try to fight an entire corps off one road.
GEN. HORROCKS, COMMANDER BRITISH XXX CORPS
TO GENERAL 'GENTLEMAN JIM' GAVIN, COMMANDER US 82ND AB

By now the Guards and the Airborne Troopers were fighting off constant German counter-attacks on the key road to Arnhem, which the Americans had re-named 'Hell's Highway'. For both Allies, it was the heaviest fighting of the war. But both the Guards and the Airborne were thin on the ground and as far as the latter were concerned they had little in the way of heavy weapons to fight off the German armoured attacks. Once Taylor's own CP was under tank attack and although the German assault was fought off at the cost of two Panthers knocked out, again the British traffic edging its way northwards to the relief of the surrounded 'Red Devils' was stalled and held up.

Still the Americans were not impressed by the fighting prowess of the 'Micks', the Irish Guards. Naturally the former didn't realise that the British had suffered great losses in Normandy and had been forced to 'cannibalise' two infantry divisions to find reinforcements for the other fighting divisions. Soon Churchill would call up 250,000 key factory workers, up to the age of forty-five, to fill the gaps in his infantry and in the case of the Irish Guards, they had been forced to accept second line troops from the RAF Regiment and AA Artillery to make up their numbers; and most of them were not even 'Micks'!

The 101st was running out of fighting men, too. In one case, Bob Gramche of the 'Screaming Eagles', who had been badly wounded, tried to make up the numbers in his depleted outfit by propping up dead Germans around his defensive position, as if they were 'Ami' paratroopers. He received the Silver Star for that piece of resourcefulness in a desperate situation. He lived to receive it.

In another, Private Bernard Sterno, who had been wounded four times in Normandy, smuggled himself aboard a re-supply transport bound for the fighting zone. When the pilot was over the DZ, Sterno jumped and found his old outfit.

> First Sergeant Bush promoted me to buck sergeant on the spot. They needed squad leaders because of all the casualties. The guys I knew were all around all talking to me. One guy said, "We killed a lot of Germans". About half our guys were wounded or dead. We weren't too many left.
>
> PRIVATE STERNO, 101ST AB

So the new 'buck sergeant' went off to war. But this time his luck had run out for good. He and some fellow troopers bumped into a German patrol which outnumbered them. He was hit again and captured. Sterno did manage to escape once for six days by jumping out of a POW train, but he was recaptured and fated to spend the rest of the war 'in the bag' ...

And still the fighting continued. September gave way to October and although the surviving 'Red Devils' had been evacuated secretly over the Rhine, the battle continued. Now the 'Screaming Eagles' were battling at the side of the men of the Duke of Cornwall's Light Infantry belonging to General Thomas' 43rd Infantry Division. This was a formation that, led by 'Butcher' Thomas, suffered a complete one hundred per cent turn-round in personnel in the campaign, including all its battalion commanders killed or wounded in action: a terrible record that even the 101st couldn't match.[16]

The British Army had no dash or vigour... When a lead tank or armoured car was hit or 'brewed up', their armoured units seldom seemed to react or manoeuvre the way American armour responded... British infantry - excellent fighters, tough to dislodge if they didn't want to go. However, I suspect that many priggish officers and class-conscious ways mitigated against effective relationships with their men.

CAPT. LADD, 502ND PARACHUTE INFANTRY REGIMENT STAFF

The outstanding parachute battalion action of the war.'

GEN. GAVIN, 82ND AB, SPEAKING OF 2ND BATTALION, BRITISH PARACHUTE REGIMENT, SEPT. '44

In essence, it seems in retrospect that General Horrocks could have succeeded in covering the sixty-odd miles to Arnhem from the start line on schedule. Thanks to the 'Screaming Eagles' of the 101st AB, the road was open. But the Guards Armoured Division had halted that first night at Valkenswaard. Thus it was that a quicker start was not made on the replacing of the bridge at Son.

In addition, if the bridge over the Waal at Nijmegen had been seized with the same speed as that over the Maas was, then Horrocks XXX Corps would have reached Betuwe in thirty-six hours. It could have then tackled the final leg of the drive to Arnhem before the 10th SS Panzer Division had crossed with more armour and Panzer grenadiers at the Pannerden Ferry to stop the British advance.

It is possible that for once Horrocks' enthusiasm was not transmitted adequately to those who served under him and it may have been that some of his more junior officers and NCOs did not fully comprehend the problem and importance of speed.

GEN. URQUART, COMMANDER 1ST BATTALION AB DIVISION

At all events, although the two US airborne divisions had successfully carried out their missions, the overall operation had been a failure. The British had suffered 13,226 casualties, the Americans 3,974. Of these General Taylor's 101st AB had incurred a loss of 2,118 men killed, wounded, taken prisoner. In essence, the losses at Arnhem had been fifty per cent more than had been suffered on D-Day. For what? As someone remarked bitterly at the time - 'a sixty mile highway heading to nowhere'.

Thus it ended in failure, accusation and counter-accusation. There'd be no victory by Christmas. The 'boys' wouldn't be going home for the festive season after all. Instead the 'Screaming Eagles' were now fated to face their greatest challenge yet - the 'Battle of Bastogne'.

V

BASTOGNE

In the early winter of 1944, the 'Screaming Eagles' were in the Top Brass's bad books. Eisenhower, in particular, was angry with the survivors of the action in Holland. This after the failure of Montgomery's 'Market Garden' operation, the 101st was not sent back to its stamping grounds in England. In retrospect, many of the Division's friends in that country were probably glad they weren't.

After seventy-two days in combat since 6th June 1944, and with over six thousand men killed, wounded, captured or missing, the 'Screaming Eagles' had become, in part, an ill-disciplined, angry outfit that didn't take to orders from above, especially if they were regarded as 'chicken shit'. In short, in their new base in France at the old French cavalry barracks complex at Mourmelon near the world's champagne capital of Rheims, they had gotten out of hand.

> E [Eisenhower] discussed with him [his chief-of-staff] the discipline of 101st and 82nd Airborne Divisions. It is bad, numerous cases of rape, looting, strong measures will have to be taken. E suggests that there should be a public hanging, particularly in the case of rape.
> KAY SUMMERSBY, EISENHOWER'S DRIVER/SECRETARY 6TH NOV. 1944

Those seventy-two days in the line in Holland, plus the D-Day landings had certainly taken their toll. Already a staff sergeant and an officer on Gen. Taylor's staff had committed suicide by blowing their brains out. A fourth of the division had been knocked out, including three of the four regimental commanders. Now the camp was flooded with callow replacements from the States and although training was back in full swing, the heart seemed to have gone from many of those who were doing the training. Indeed some of the veterans couldn't take the strain. Instead, however, blowing their brains out, they simply seized the chance offered them, now that the battle was over, and transferred out.

> Mental strain and physical drain had caught up with them at last after the haven of Camp Mourmelon was reached.
> FRED MACKENZIE, THE ONLY REPORTER TO ACCOMPANY THE 101ST AB
> THROUGH THE BASTOGNE BATTLE

'The days of flash and dash,' Colonel Ewell told his men as he took command of the 501st Parachute Regiment, after its commander, 'Geronimo' Johnson had been killed in Holland, 'are over'. Most of his men thought so too. Now they hoped for refurbishment - a lengthy one - before being sent into the line in a reserve position. Why, Colonel Sink, commander of 506th Parachute Infantry Regiment, was going on Christmas leave and General Taylor had been summoned to Washington for that same period of time; (later the Division, as a whole, would never forgive him for that absence); the men were beginning to save rations and booze for a Christmas binge. So, all in all, if the Top Brass weren't impressed with the 101st, the 'Screaming Eagles' weren't impressed by the generals and their fancy flunkeys in Versailles, Paris, France. They would have a damned good rest and enjoy Christmas. They'd worry about what was to come then in 1945. It was going to be a pious hope, as we will see. The 'Krauts' had other plans for the men of the 101st Airborne Division ...

Just before dawn on the morning of Saturday 16th December 1944, strange things were happening along the length of the River Our, the border river between Luxembourg and Germany. In the freezing darkness, dark shapes were seen wading through the shallows where the Americans had crossed into the Reich three months before, in what now seemed another age, before being repulsed with a bloody nose. Others were using underwater bridges copied from the Russians.[18] A few were trying the wooden bridge, secretly constructed and erected, with muffled hammers only hours before. Everywhere was silent hectic activity as hundreds of infantrymen started to climb the steep wooded height beyond to reach what the 'Amis' called the 'Skyline Drive', the main ridge road connecting the Luxembourg capital with the nearest Belgian town of any size, St. Vith.

Here the road was held in a series of fortified villages along it by the 110 US Infantry Regiment, part of the battered 28th US Infantry Division, recently returned from the 'Hell of the Hurtgen Forest', where the 28th had suffered five thousand casualties.

In one of these villages, Hosingen, a lone sentry, was posted at the top of the local water tower. Here in daylight the sentry could overlook the whole of the valley of the Our below, up to the heights, which hid the Siegfried Line. Before he had taken up his post, he had been warned by his company commander, Lt. Feiker, fated to die violently before the week was out, to be careful. There was a lot of funny things happening in the no-man's land below and the locals, who spoke German and had relatives in the Wehrmacht, had suddenly begun to react against the 'Yanks', as if they didn't want it to be known that they associated with them. Besides the company stationed at Hosingen was on its own; the nearest other Americans were a good two miles away.

So the young sentry on top of the tower to the right of the road leading to St. Vith (it's still there), sweated it out, stamping his frozen feet and probably thinking of the cup of steaming hot 'java' waiting for him on relief.

But that day, the unknown young soldier, one of the three thousand odd of the 110th Infantry who would succumb to what was soon to come, was not fated to enjoy that coffee. At five-thirty that Saturday dawn, which changed the history of Western Europe, he called down by telephone to report to his worried superior. He had seen 'pinpoints of light' everywhere below. For a second or two he must have been at a loss to explain them. Down at the Our, the lights seemed to spread the length of the curve of the border river at that spot. A moment later and his ears were assailed by the belching thunder of a huge enemy artillery barrage: 554 cannon of General von Luettwitz's 47th Panzer Corps had just opened fire on the 110th Infantry's positions along the 'Skyline Drive'. The Battle of the Bulge, American's Gettysburg of the 20th Century had begun. The race for Bastogne had commenced ...

In reality we don't know what *really* happened at Eisenhower's HQ at Versailles that late afternoon when the news of the attack into the Ardennes finally reached Shaef. The three main witnesses to the event, Generals Eisenhower, Bradley and Strong (Ike's chief-of-intelligence) were all compromised before the Battle of the Bulge and fudged the facts afterwards for obvious reasons. Bradley called it a 'spoiling attack'. At all events they continued to celebrate Ike's fifth star, just granted him by Congress, and enjoy the last Saturday before Christmas. They played poker and enjoyed the rare treat of a bottle of good Scotch, 'Highland Piper', presented to Ike by another general.

One thing we know for certain about that Saturday that could well have meant the end of the careers of the two Americans and the one Scot, if others hadn't picked the chestnuts out of the fire for them, is the two military decisions made at the time. One was to send the 7th Armoured Division from Holland to the general area of St. Vith, the major road-and-rail centre of the area under attack. The other was to release Ike's only infantry reserve, the 82nd and 101st Airborne Divisions, recently returned from Holland and about up to seventy per cent of their enlisted man official strength. But where was the latter division to be sent?

It was an obscure British officer on Eisenhower's staff who came up with the answer. He was named Whiteley, Colonel Whiteley, a man totally unknown among those many who have made a study of what some maintain is the key battle of the Bulge. Whiteley had studied the area and terrain around Bastogne prior to the battle. Now he suggested to Strong, that after St. Vith, Bastogne should be reinforced and held (Patton, in contrast, thought two days later that Bastogne should be abandoned). Together they took the idea to Bedell Smith, Ike's fiery, bad-tempered chief-of-staff 'somebody's got to be a son-of-a-bitch around here!' The latter agreed and the decision was made.

Pardon my French, Lev, but where in hell has this sonuvabitch gotten all his strength?
GEN. BRADLEY TO MAJOR GENERAL ALLEN ON THE GERMAN 'SURPRISE
ATTACK'
17TH DEC. 1944

That Sunday, 17th December, the 'Screaming Eagles' place in the history books of war in the 20th Century was decided ...

The morning of Monday, 18th December dawned grey and misty. The men were sombre and low-voiced in the mess halls and squad huts of the 101st's Camp Mourmelon. They had been alerted for the move into the unknown. Now they waited for their transport. When it came around mid-day, they were surprised. This time they wouldn't fly into battle, as paratroopers should. Instead, just like at Slapton Sands, they'd be taken there by truck - great big open ten-tonners - in which, they opined, they'd 'freeze our nuts off'. They were right.

Already key officers were ahead of them, driving the historic routes taken by armies so often before them - Verdun, Sedan, Luxembourg. They passed elements of the 82nd AB, also looking for the best routes in a confused rear area, where no one seemed to know what was going on and the little snowbound villages and townships held by the Americans were filled with conflicting and frightening rumours. Americans were fleeing to the rear everywhere, too.

Sir, unless these people are having a premature case of the jitters, I'll say the Germans must be barrelling this way fast.' 'So I was thinking. We'll soon find out.
CONVERSATION BETWEEN COL. KINNARD AND GEN. MCAULIFFE, 18TH DEC.
1944

As the two senior officers drove into the outskirts of Bastogne looking for the office of Gen. Middleton, the VIII Corps Commander, they realised that it wasn't just the jitters; the front had broken. What they were seeing was what was left of the 110th Regiment, plus stragglers from the ill-fated 106 Infantry Division, which, after five days in the line, were surrounded, with two regiments of its green infantrymen about to surrender; and men from half a dozen other outfits. All of them heading for the River Meuse to the rear and what they believed was safety beyond the Belgian river.

Middleton was in a difficult situation. Not only had his corps' front broken with the Germans of General von Luettwitz's Panzerkorps flooding through the gap, heading for Clervaux and then Bastogne, driving for their primary objective, the River Meuse; but he was also plagued by a gaggle of generals. They were all of different ranks and all eager to use rank to take over command of Bastogne while he, Middleton, pulled his corps HQ back to nearby Neufchateau. Indeed in some cases, it came to open slanging matches.

What do you know about armor, General? Maybe you want the 101st Division attached to your Combat Command, Colonel?
EXCHANGE BETWEEN COL. CHERRY OF 10TH ARMORED AND GEN. MCAULIFFE

In the end, after Middleton had refused to see Gen. Cota of the 28th Division and Gen. Gaffey of the 4th Armored withdrew his leading combat command to Neufchateau (it would take him a week of hard and bloody fighting to recover the ground he gave up in a matter of hours), Middleton left the most junior general, McAuliffe, in charge of the defence of Bastogne. Later perhaps some of the other more senior generals were glad that they had not landed that particular hot potato!

Troy, of all the goddam crazy things I ever head, leaving the 101st Airborne to be surrounded in Bastogne is the worst!
GEN. PATTON TO GEN. 'TROY' MIDDLETON, 19TH DEC. 1944

By 19th December, McAuliffe, 'the Old Crock', had established a ring defence of Belgian communications centre with its five thousand strong civilian population, famous hitherto for its annual autumn 'Nuts Fair', a fact that would lead to misunderstandings later after the German surrender offer and the supposed McAuliffe reply of 'Nuts!' Inside the defensive circle were the 101st Airborne, Combat Command B of the 10th Armored Division, the 463rd Field Artillery Battalion and stragglers from broken units of Middleton's VIII Corps.

Facing the defenders, who so far *outnumbered* their attackers, were elements of three divisions of von Luettwitz's Panzerkorps; the 2nd Viennese Panzer, the Panzerlehr (Tank Training) Division; and the 26th Volksgrenadier (People's Grenadier) Division. For the time being the latter infantry division, which had successfully forced the River Our Line and smashed the US 110th Infantry Regiment, was the 'Screaming Eagles' main opponent. Admittedly von Luettwitz was concerned with capturing Bastogne, but he wasn't going to bog down his mobile force, the 2nd and Panzerlehr Divisions, fighting in a built up area where tanks were more of a hindrance than an asset. He'd leave the reduction of Bastogne to the infantry of the 26th Volksgrenadier. His first priority was crossing the River Meuse to the west of Bastogne.

> Bastogne must be eventually taken from the rear. If it is not taken, it will always remain an ulcer on our lines of communication [to the River Meuse]... Therefore first clear out Bastogne and then carry on.
> VON LUETTWITZ TO HIS DIVISIONAL COMMANDERS, 12TH DEC. 1944

Five days after making the above statement to his subordinates, von Luettwitz realised that Bastogne was not just held by the headquarters troops of Middleton's VIII Corps, but that an elite American formation was heading for the Belgian road-and-rail centre. Due to US carelessness in their radio traffic, which was always carefully monitored by the Germans, he was able to read an 'Ami' signal - *in clear* - that the 101st was on its way to Bastogne. Immediately he ordered Bayerlein's Panzerlehr and Kokett's 26th to break off their general mopping up operations in the Clervaux area and head straight from the dying Luxembourg city and headquarters of the decimated 110th Infantry Regiment for Bastogne itself. They had to beat the 'Screaming Eagles' to the future 'Nuts City'.

But as we already know, the Americans had beaten them in that race ...

In part it was Fritz Bayerlein's fault. The commander of the Panzerlehr, who had a tremendous fighting record in Russia, North Africa and France as a tank general, seemingly allowed himself to be lured into traps of one kind or another during that dash for Bastogne. At Weiswampach, a village in Luxembourg on the route to Clervaux-Bastogne, a farmer named Jean Reckinger, supposedly a Nazi sympathiser, was asked about the road ahead. Reckinger answered Bayerlein's question with a confident 'It's a good road General, but you must turn off at the border [between Luxembourg and Belgium] to the right'. With the Corps Commander breathing down his neck, Bayerlein set off again for Bastogne. It was a terrible mistake. After a kilometre or so, the road turned into a dirt track and then disappeared altogether. For a few, but crucial hours, a whole tank column of the Panzerlehr was bogged down, unable to turn in the confused darkness and deep mud, while Bayerlein fumed impotently.

Some time afterwards Bayerlein compounded his troubles, by

unaccountably stopping for several hours to have his 'wound dressed' by a pretty blonde captured US Army nurse. It is assumed that she did more than attend to his light flesh wound. Strangely enough, neither of these two people, who, indirectly, did quite a bit to make the Germans lose the race for Bastogne, were ever found after the war. Perhaps they belonged to legends which always gather around major battles in history?

At all events the Germans lost the race and when finally the two Panzer divisions began circumventing Bastogne heading for the River Meuse, leaving the 'People's Grenadiers' to attack, the defences were in place.

You're young and by tomorrow you'll probably be nervous and you might think that it would be a good idea to withdraw. When you begin thinking that, remember that I told you it would be best *not* to withdraw until I order you to do so.

COL. ROBERTS TO MAJOR DOBRY, 10TH ARMORED DIV.
NIGHT OF SUNDAY/MONDAY 18TH/19TH DEC. '44

In command, the 'Old Crock', McAuliffe, was a general who was going to take no nonsense from either the Germans or his subordinates. The forty-six year old obscure former artillery commander of the 101st was in total command. He would take neither advice nor orders from others; in due course, even 'Blood an' Guts' Patton, feared, if admired, throughout the whole US Army, would come in for tongue-lashings by this man of destiny. While he waited for his perimeter to take shape at his HQ not far from Bastogne's 'grand rue' that icy day in December 1944, the stocky tough little paratroop commander could hardly have visualised that half a century later his own grandchildren would stand in awe as they gazed at the statue of 'grandpa', which today adorns Place McAuliffe.

But now McAuliffe had no time to consider the future. Already the defenders knew that the Krauts were on their way. They were. On Wednesday afternoon, 20th December, von Luettwitz's troops made their first attempt to rush the Ami defences, true blitzkrieg style. Using thick fog as cover, a mixed assault group of armour and Panzer Grenadiers rushed a roadblock held by combat engineers at the village of Bonoey. A protracted fight commenced. Four German half-tracks, filled with grenadiers, managed to break off the action and, heading for the next village of Marvie, hoped they had made the decisive thrust. As the angry snap-and-crack of small arms fire weakened behind them, they reasoned, they had broken the thin outer shell of the enemy defences. They were wrong. At Marvie they found out their mistake. There they were stopped too. By chance, the place was occupied. They were stopped dead. But von Luettwitz was not disheartened. Everywhere it seemed the Americans had fled or vanished. He kept up the pressure.

Now the paratroopers started to be thrown into the rough-and-ready defensive line. From Noville came the request from a team of the 10th Armored to pull out. It was denied. Major Dobry, in charge there, was ordered to hold on as long as possible. The 'Screaming Eagles' were on their way.

Hurriedly the 1st Battalion of the 506th Parachute Infantry was flung into the battle. On their route of march, ammunition, bazookas and other weapons were handed out to the troops, many of them who were without weapons. Still they were used to this sort of confusion in Normandy and Holland. They grabbed what they could and continued on the way to their own personal date with destiny.

But as they got closer to the scene of the action, they passed scores and then hundreds of retreating US troops. They were 'bugging out' in near panic, many recklessly moving to the west in tanks and half-tracks, threatening to run down anyone who attempted to stop them. Here and there an unarmed or lightly armed 'Screaming Eagle' tried to beg a weapon from the retreating men. To no avail. They were stopping for nothing and nobody. One paratrooper waving a tree branch, it is recorded, swore: 'I'm gonna get me a Mauser rifle by evening'. Whether he did or not, it is unfortunately not recorded. Perhaps he was dead by then.

> You'll never stop 'em boys... We're going to have a try at it, sir.
> CONVERSATION BETWEEN LYLE SNYDER, 101ST AB
> AND AN UNKNOWN MAJOR FLEEING FROM THE FRONT

Thus they pushed forward, 'new boys' and the 'vets', armed and unarmed. Some of them had fought the Germans before and won; others had yet to fire a shot in anger. There were those among them, who didn't even know the country in which they were.[19] Most of them had never heard of Bastogne, even most of their junior officers hadn't. Indeed General McAuliffe and three of his regional commanders had never been within fifty miles of Bastogne; only one regimental commander had taken a short leave in the area of the future 'Nuts City' and 'walked the ground'. What they were going to defend to the last. But defend it they were going to do.

Take a good look at the name on that sign [Bastogne] because we're gonna make history.

JIM 'PEE WEE' MARTIN, 506 PARACHUTE INFANTRY REGIMENT

On the same day that the paratroopers marched on Noville to take up the German challenge, the Allied Top Brass (minus Field Marshal Montgomery, who, as we will see, had plans of his own) met at the 18th century Maginot Caserne under the bloody heights of Verdun, where in that great blood-letting of 1916, both General de Gaulle and Adolf Hitler had fought. Ushered into a freezing squad room, warmed by a single pot-bellied stove, the generals under Eisenhower assembled to discuss what should be done about the thirty-mile deep German 'surprise' breakthrough in the Ardennes. Again all who were present at Verdun that Tuesday were prejudiced and compromised so their testimony must be regarded as tainted. So let us stick to the two main decisions which emerged from the impromptu conference. The first was that the Ardennes front would have two separate commanders: General Bradley in the South with his headquarters at Luxembourg City. In essence, all that Bradley would have under his command from the three US Armies he had been commanding was what was left of Middleton's VIII Corps and Patton's Third Army. Now Patton was ordered to turn round three of his divisions and start them off northwards to meet the Bulge threat.

There was a stir, shuffling of feet, as those present straightened up in their chairs... in some faces skepticism. But through the room the current of excitement leapt like a flame. To disengage three divisions actually in combat and launch them over more than a hundred miles of icy roads, straight into the heart of a major attack of unprecedented violence presented problems which few commanders would have taken to resolve in that length of time.

COLONEL CODMAN, PATTON'S AIDE, VERDUN 19TH DEC.1944

Although the US official line was that the Ardennes attack came as a complete surprise, it is significant that Patton had ordered his staff to study the possibility of moving part of his army to the north into the US 1st Army sector on 12th December, i.e. *four* days before the start of the German 'surprise' attack and *seven* before Eisenhower gave him the order to do so.[20]

The second decision that Montgomery would be given command of the north flank of the German Bulge, thus taking over both the US 1st and 9th Armies (i.e. most of the US troops in the area) would be the most controversial and would be kept secret till January 1945 when the German threat was over. Not that Montgomery, 'the little Limey fart', as Patton called him scornfully, cared. In his usual high-handed manner, he had *already* taken over command of the 1st US Army the day before; and without Ike's permission.

Already Montgomery was rushing troops to the River Meuse to make a last stand there (he had already summoned the 101st's old sparring partners, the British 6th Airborne Division from Britain to Belgium). Montgomery's aim was to stop the German Army crossing there, west of Bastogne.

And that was goodbye to our Christmas tuck-in. We'd swapped compo rations [the standard British Army ration] for Belgie beer and ham, organised extra sugar and raisins for the Christmas pud - even the officers and sergeants had volunteered to give up their spirit ration for the big Christmas blow out to come. But that wasn't to be. Monty spoke. The call came and we were off into the bloody blue - minus our Christmas dinner. All I ate that Christmas was a stale cheese wad - and it was frozen bloody solid as well!

PRIVATE EVANS, BRITISH 53RD INF. DIV.

Thus it was, almost by chance and the dictates of local geography, that virtually all of the American forces, plus Monty's XXX Corps of the Arnhem fiasco, were concentrated in the general region of that hitherto obscure Belgian township of Bastogne.

But before the counter-attack would get underway a lot would happen, and for the time being everything depended upon just how long the men of McAuliffe's 101st - 'the Battered Bastard of Bastogne', as their PR man would soon be calling them - truthfully this time - could hang on. Now the 'Screaming Eagles' were about to be subjected to their greatest ordeal of World War Two.

VI

BASTOGNE II

By Thursday 21st December 1944, two days before the Third Army's relief attack was due to kick off, the 101st Airborne and the other US formation trapped inside Bastogne were beginning to suffer badly. In the cellars of the houses grouped around the main square and the makeshift hospitals spread about 'Nuts City', there were 1,500 serious casualties; and, it must be admitted, a goodly number of frightened GIs who wouldn't or couldn't fight. By now the harassed Airborne medics were beginning to use captured German paper bandages instead of cloth, to dress their comrades' wounds. In one case an enterprising US doctor engaged a number of Belgian women to wash stained bandages so that they could be used again on the lightly wounded. The modern day 'Florence Nightingales' were paid for their unpleasant and sometimes dangerous tasks in 'Luckies' and 'Camels'. Cigarettes - as yet - were not in short supply, but everything else was.

Outside the dead were left unburied, covered in mounds of new snow, lying unrecorded among the shattered American vehicles. For the German Luftwaffe, which as far as the 'Screaming Eagles' were concerned, had not made much of an appearance during the campaign so far, was making more frequent tip-and-run bombing raids. The Germans obviously knew from their reconnaissance parties and their agents within the besieged town (for there are persistent rumours that the enemy had managed to infiltrate spies into Bastogne) that the 'Amis' had no flak to speak of. The numerous notices posted in the main square and along the shattered main street of Bastogne along which Hitler himself had ridden proudly four years before just after the capture of the Belgian town, showed that morale was beginning to weaken in some quarters. For they announced with brutal simplicity that looters would be shot without trial. All in all, everything seemed to be going in the Germans' favour.

But there was one faint shimmer of hope on the horizon. The bad weather - the Germans had called it happily 'Führer Weather' - had started to clear. It was growing noticeably colder. The heavy clouds were beginning to thin and the hard-pressed fighting men shivering in their foxholes on both sides knew what that meant. Soon the mighty Allied bombing forces in Britain which had been partially grounded since 16th December by the bad weather would be able to fly again. Von Luettwitz realised that he had to deal with the 'running sore' of Bastogne before the feared Allied jabos (dive-bombers) came winging in in their scores, their hundreds. Back in Normandy he had seen his own 2nd Panzer Division, which he had then commanded, shattered by the rocket-firing Typhoons and Mustangs. He didn't want that to happen again. He had to act fast.

Thus it was that just before twelve noon on Friday 22nd December, men of the 101st's Gliderborne Infantry manning a roadblock at Marvie, were amazed to see four German soldiers walking slowly and hesitantly down the road from Arlon in Luxembourg. One of them was carrying a white flag. Were the Germans coming to surrender?

They weren't. Three Yanks went out to meet them and one of the Germans, who spoke English, asked to see an American officer. They were taken to the command post of the glider infantry company involved (it's still there). From here the news that German emissaries had arrived, complete with white flags, went up the chain of command. The news spread to the troopers. They too thought that the Germans had come to surrender. It was recorded that many of the weary dirty GIs got out of their holes, shaved and gave themselves a 'cat's lick' and prepared to have their photographs taken when the US Signal Corps' cameraman came to record the momentous event. They were going to be sorely disappointed. The siege of Bastogne and the accompanying slaughter were not over yet - by a long chalk!

Finally the 'surrender' group arrived at 101st's Airborne HQ in the Bastogne's brownstone army barracks, which in the last four years had been occupied by the Belgian, German and now American armies. Here the 101st's acting Chief-of-Staff, Colonel Moore, looked at the two sheets of paper: one in German and one in English. Both had been typed on a captured Belgian or American typewriter (the German version lacked the 'umlaut', the two dots over vowel sounds common in German), but both had the same threat: 'surrender or else'.

There is only one possibility to save the encircled USA troops from total annihilation: that is the honourable surrender of the encircled town. In order to think it over a term of two hours will be granted... If this proposal should be rejected, one German Artillery Corps and six heavy AA Battalions are ready to annihilate the USA troops in and near Bastogne. The order for firing will be given immediately after this two hours' term.
ENGLISH TRANSLATION OF VON LUETTWITZ'S ULTIMATUM, 22:12:44[21]

Moore roused McAuliffe from a nap. The acting commander of the 101st was feeling the strain; after all he was twice the age of his young troopers. He heard Moore out and then in that typical 'Old Crock' manner of his, snapped: 'Oh shit!' and promptly went to sleep once more.

Impatiently the Germans waited for an answer. They knew that Luettwitz was bluffing. He didn't have the men for a full-scale attack on Bastogne and the six flak battalions existed only in his imagination. But they knew, too, the 'Amis' were having their own problems. As usual the Americans were very careless in their wireless communications and the Germans were reading their urgent demands for air re-supply and bomber strikes to make up for their lack of artillery etc. etc.

They asked their temporary captors what their General's reply to their surrender request was. The deadline - two o'clock that grey December afternoon - was nearing rapidly. In the end they convinced Colonel Kinnard of the 101st to return to McAuliffe and ask for his answer to von Luettwitz's ultimatum.

McAuliffe, who naturally wouldn't even dream of surrendering, was half asleep still and not very articulate, said to Kinnard: 'I don't know what to tell them'. According to the 'sanitized' version released to McAuliffe's troopers two days later on Christmas Eve 1944 (and naturally to an admiring Western World, too), Kinnard suggested, 'How about that first remark of yours?'

Patton might have got away with the crudity. After all, the day he crossed the Rhine, he signalled Eisenhower, 'Today I *pissed* in the Rhine'. But not McAuliffe. 'Shit' was changed to 'Nuts': the word was homely, typically American and could be used in front of anyone's prim and proper grandma without making her blush even faintly.

> 22nd December
> To the German Commander
>   NUTS!
> The American Commander
>
> THE MCAULIFFE REPLY NOTE

That one word 'Nuts' puzzled the German surrender delegation greatly. They asked: "Is that reply a negative or affirmative?"

Colonel Harper, who brought the Germans' McAuliffe's note snapped, "If you continue the attack, we will kill every goddam German soldier that tries to break into the city".

The Germans were not impressed by the threat. They saluted and answered, "And we will kill many Americans. That is war".

"On your way, Bud", Harper growled without returning the salute and then before he could stop himself and for no reason he could explain afterwards, added a friendly, "Good Luck!..."

Thus the great Bastogne legend was born. It has entered American history, together with such evocative and key phrases as 'damn the torpedoes', 'we have just begun to fight', 'praise the Lord and pass the ammunition'; all those emotive statements which made young men - and women - proud enough of their country and forefathers to go out to new wars and try to emulate them.

But for most Europeans, not only the German peace emissaries, it meant nothing. As we have seen, the Belgians at Bastogne thought it referred in some vague way to the town's annual autumn nuts fair. The British opined it was a typical brash piece of Americanism. Even Hemingway, who was currently on his way to join the 4th Infantry Division in the Bulge, scoffed at it as a product of the '101st's Calypso-singing PR man'. Be that as it may, the legend had been born. Now all that the 'Battered Bastards of Bastogne', as that same PR man with his guitar was calling the 101st's hard-pressed troopers dug in on the place's perimeter, needed or wanted was a hero: the Seventh Cavalry galloping in to the rescue. That would round off the legend. *Where was 'Ole Blood an' Guts' Patton?*

Everyone in this Army understands that we are not fighting this battle in any half-cocked manner. It's either root-hog or die! Shoot the works. If those Hun bastards can do it then so can we. If those sons-of-bitches want war in the raw, then that is the way we'll give it to them.

PATTON FIRST ORDER OF THE DAY, 24TH DECEMBER 1944

Patton was a 'prima donna' among an Army of prima donnas holding the rank of general. But Patton always made quite sure that no one else took the credit for any victory achieved under his command. When he took over the US 2nd Corps after its defeat at the Battle of the Kasserine Pass in 1943, he used a battle-experienced British tank brigadier to shape up his defeated tankers. No one ever learned that fact; not even his biographers. As soon as any one of his subordinate commanders appeared to be grabbing for the headlines, Patton ensured he was transferred, 'kicked upstairs', to a higher command on the other side of the Atlantic, went on sick leave etc. Etc. Barrel-chested General Wood, commander of his brilliant Fourth Armored Division in the early stages of the campaign, was a typical example. In short, Patton wanted mediocre staff, servile divisional commanders and tame formations under his command, who were prepared to fight and die, if necessary, without making claims on individual glory or recognition. As far as General Patton was concerned, it was sufficient that they were serving in 'Patton's Third Army' - that was surely glory enough.

So, we can assume, that Patton was neither interested in Bastogne nor the 101st Airborne as such. We have already seen that he felt that Bastogne should have been abandoned and that Middleton was a fool to have gotten himself surrounded in the place in the first instant. As for the 101st Airborne, Patton didn't believe in formations, elite or otherwise, which would spend a short time in battle, suffer high casualties and then retire to bathe in whatever glory they had achieved during the brief spell of combat. He wanted men in the line all the time - men he could count on in his future planning. It was probably for that reason that he was the first commander to accept black fighting men in a still strictly segregated US Army, in particular artillery-men and tankers, when no one else wanted them. He'd tell them, using the same old spiel, that when their grand-kids asked them what they'd done in the 'big war', they'd be able to reply that they hadn't 'shovelled shit in Louisiana', but 'had killed Krauts with Patton's Third Army'. This breaking of the traditional military colour bar had nothing to do with liberal sentiments, but was strictly a reflection of Patton's insatiable desire for 'bodies'.

Naturally Patton was right. Capable, clever generals who fought not just battles, but campaigns, needed to know what they could count on in the way of 'bodies'. Montgomery ran his army on the same basis. Let inferior commanders concern themselves with what the traditionalists regarded as flashy, fly-by-night outfits, such as commanders, rangers, paratroopers. What a real army commander needed was a simple, stolid footslogger - the 'PBI' (the 'Poor Bloody Infantry'). *They'd* stay in the line until the campaign was won - or they were taken out of it, feet first!

One day after von Luettwitz tried to trick McAuliffe into surrendering Bastogne (and was roundly taken to task by his army commander von Manteuffel for having done so) Patton commenced his counter-attack towards the Belgian township. His plan envisaged a three-division assault. In the main spot was Patton's elite Fourth Armored Division, which had previously withdrawn from Bastogne when it had been thought not worth defending. It would roll up from Luxembourg in the south. Starting at the Luxembourg border town of Arlon, it would use the limited road network to strike for Bastogne. On the right flank, attacking through the rolling hill country of that part of Luxembourg, the 4th Armored would be supported by two infantry divisions in line abreast: the 80th and 26th Infantry, both battle-experienced and capable formations. Although the weather and terrain were against this three divisional assault, it seemed that it would soon speedily break through to a besieged Bastogne; after all the attackers greatly outnumbered the German defenders of the area.

For facing them and the 4th's massed armour was one single German infantry division, with no armour of its own, save for some forty self-propelled guns.

Proudly the Germans of this single division, holding the line south of Bastogne called themselves 'The Green Devils', the name bestowed once on Germany's elite parachute corps. But that one division, the Fifth Fallschirmjager-division, was an airborne division in name only.

They were a fourth-line division in reality. In my opinion the 5th Para should have never been allowed across the borders of the Reich. All the same my 'boys' did give the Americans a nasty surprise.

GEN. HEILMANN, LAST COMMANDER FIFTH GERMAN PARACHUTE DIVISION
AFTER THE WAR

The Fifth which had been wiped out in France was now composed of culls from the Luftwaffe and German Navy, built around a handful of wounded veterans and former paras who had survived the holocaust of St. Lo and the retreat from France. Hardly any of its company commanders had undergone parachute training and only one of its three regimental commanders was a trained Fallschirmjager. As for the men, they had undergone a rapid one-month conversion course into infantrymen and indeed some of them were still wearing bits and pieces of Navy and Air Force clothing when they went into action. Apart from a handful of hurriedly organised old-fashioned SP guns, the Division crossed the River Sauer to block Patton's counter-attack from the south using transport as old as warfare itself - namely horses and carts.

Heilmann, its commander then a colonel and a highly decorated veteran of the Italian Monte Cassino in the summer of 1944, must have despaired at the state of his 10,000 strong new division. Privately he considered it a 'fourth class formation', but he kept his doubts to himself. Heavily built with a pugnacious jaw, he was a fighter in the true airborne tradition. The Fifth had been given a job to do; they would do it. But just how well they would do so, came as a surprise even to that veteran of nearly five years of combat on three continents. Soon Heilmann's young paras (in name only) would make nonsense of Patton's boast to Eisenhower that he would be in Bastogne within forty-eight hours of the start of his counter-attack.

On Christmas Eve 1944, Bastogne was outwardly peaceful. The 'battered bastards of Bastogne' (the guitar-playing PR officer had gone overboard in his description of the hard-pressed 'Eagles'), were nearly exhausted as were the supplies of certain types of ammunition, such as mortar bombs. The 'Eagles' were tense, too. They had encircled for a week now. Every day new rumours had swept the perimeter about Patton's arrival. But despite 'Ole Blood an' Guts' promise, they had still not been relieved. Heilmann's young culls were making the Fourth fight hard for every yard of ground gained - and the coldest winter for Europe for a quarter of a century wasn't helping much.

Two days before, hope had been sparked in Bastogne when the garrison received the signal which stated simply but very significantly for the trapped 'Eagles', 'HUGH IS COMING!' Hugh was the new commander of the Fourth Armored, General Hugh Gaffey, recently transferred from Patton's staff to a field command 'to give him battle experience'. But HUGH had failed to make an appearance that day. Indeed HUGH was further away from Bastogne than he had been at the start of the breakthrough operations.

Even McAuliffe, the aged fire-eater, who had once had his tommy gun taken away from him by the divisional commander because not only was he a danger to the 'Krauts', but also to his own men, started to despair (though he never showed it). At Middleton's CP, McAuliffe told the former corps commander that Christmas Eve, "the finest present for Christmas the 101st could get would be the relief tomorrow". "I know, boy", Middleton agreed somberly, "I know".

Now both generals knew better than anyone else that the defenders and the 3,500 civilians trapped with them were at the end of their mental and physical tether.[22] Allied air supplies had helped with the ration and surgical shortages admittedly. But the soldiers and civilians were still being bombed and shelled by the Germans with little available to ward off these nerve-racking attacks. Indeed most of the defenders, who could, had retreated to the fetid, overcrowded cellars. Here and there some of the paras simply could not stand the strain. They had gone mad, been 'section-eighted' and physically restrained in primitive straitjackets.

Colonel Kinnard, who wrote the division's Christmas greeting for McAuliffe, later stated: 'We never felt that we would be overrun. We were beating back everything they threw at us. We had the houses and we were warm. They were outside the town in the snow and cold'. The comments of the survivors were unprintable. One veteran whose Christmas dinner was 'five white beans and a cup of cold broth' snarled: 'What battle was he in?'

We are giving our country and our loved ones at home a worthy Christmas present and being privileged to take part in this gallant feat of arms and are truly making for ourselves a merry Christmas.

COLONEL KINNARD, CHRISTMAS EVE 1944

That echo of Bing Crosby's current hit, *I'm Dreaming of a White Christmas* might have gone down well with the folks back home - it had a sufficiently convincing Norman Rockwell quality about it - but it left a bad taste in the mouths of the fighting 'Eagles'. The picture later in the *Stars and Stripes* of McAuliffe, Kinnard and the rest of the Division's staff sitting around a Christmas tree in a secure cellar, presumably celebrating the feast of goodwill to all men, didn't help matters either. But there was nothing much they could do about the Brass's little propaganda games. They concentrated on surviving and if they prayed that Christmas Eve, it was for a speedy German defeat and a Patton breakthrough ...

But now Patton started to put some fire behind his counter-attack. He knew, with the US forces on the defensive everywhere in the 'Bulge', he would hit the headlines in the States if he managed to relieve Bastogne; and there was nothing more he craved than headlines. He applied the pressure on his commanders and his troops, who were fighting in truly appalling conditions. Before the weather closed in, he demanded and got the support of two tactical airforces, American and British, as well as 'Bomber' Harris' heavy bombers and those of the US 8th Air Force from Britain. Together they plastered the immediate front and from there right back to the German supply bases, rail and road communication networks, west of the River Rhine.

That night, I chanced to look back from outside by CP, staring eastwards, and was shocked. Fires ranged all the way to what would be the frontier of the Reich. It was a sea of flames.

COLONEL HEILMANN, CHRISTMAS EVE 1944

Patton's assault started to pick up. The Third Army commander threw in everything he had, including completely green formations such as the US 11th Armored Division, straight from the UK. It suffered accordingly and within days its divisional commander was secretly relieved for incompetence, which wasn't the case; he simply hadn't expected to be thrown into this kind of battle in his first combat command. Heilmann's men tried their damnedest to hold up Patton's three divisional attack. But they were no match for the weight of the opposition and Patton's tremendous drive.

How Heilmann's supply lines had been finally cut. No reinforcements were coming through to fill the gaps in the ranks of the 5th Parachute Division. The weather took its toll too. Now men on both sides were fighting really to survive and to get a roof over their heads for the night and a fire to thaw them out.

In the lead now, there were two combat commands of the Fourth Armored, the best mechanised formation in the whole of the Third Army. Opposing one of these, numbering 2,500 men and their hundred odd tanks, Heilmann could muster just a single company of paras and three self-propelled guns. Heilmann appealed desperately for help. The Luftwaffe attempted to fly a low-level fighter-bomber attack on the Fourth's armoured columns. Without much success. To help Heilmann, while he was still capable of holding off the relief force, Kokott, commanding the 26th People's Grenadier Division, made a desperate three-pronged attack on Bastogne. It failed. Patton's pace quickened.

I phoned General Manteuffel. I told him I couldn't watch two fronts at once and that I didn't think the 5th Parachute could hold... and that I was in no position to prevent a breakthrough.[23] He told me to forget the 4th Armored. It, the Fourth, was quiet at the moment.

GENERAL KOKOTT

It wasn't! Just as he had once ridden his polo ponies very hard on the polo fields of pre-war USA, Patton dug his spurs in cruelly. He threatened, cajoled, praised anything to keep his relief columns moving. More and more of the 3rd Army's subordinate commanders were dismissed for tardiness. Men died of heart attacks through excessive strain, as well as by enemy bullets. Frostbite was almost endemic among the infantry. Time and time again, Patton's infantry were drawn into traps, apparently easily capturing a village and hurrying to find shelter for the night against the raging snowstorms, only to find themselves attacked by cunningly hidden German assault groups of self-propelled guns and paras. Still they pressed on.

The fighting in Bastogne had blazed up once more, too. On the night of Christmas Eve/Christmas Day, the Germans attacked yet again. They came from the *west* this time, hoping to catch the Americans waiting for an assault from the usual direction, east, by surprise. They did - for a while. For a while the 'Eagles' of the 502nd were engaged in house-to-house fighting in places such as the village of Champs. For three hours the battle rage back and forth in Champs until at six o'clock on the day of days, Christmas morning, the 502nd counter-attacked. They fought for two hours to clear out the enemy, counting ninety-nine Germans dead and three times that number wounded and captured in the process.

> Let the world never see such a Christmas night again. To die far from one's children, one's wife and mother under fire of guns, there is no greater cruelty... Life can only be for love and respect. At the sight of ruins, of blood and death, universal fraternity will arise. A German Officer.
>
> MESSAGE LEFT BEHIND BY AN UNKNOWN GERMAN OFFICER ON THE BLACKBOARD OF THE VILLAGE SCHOOL AT CHAMPS, CHRISTMAS DAY 1944

But the battle wasn't all one-sided. To the south of Champs, a large German tank force supported by infantry, presumably from the newly-arrived 15 Panzergrenadier Division, broke through the American lines. The colonel in charge was forced to make a run for it. He reached the 502nd's lines only by the skin of his teeth, almost being shot down by his own people.

Here the men of the 463rd Parachute Artillery took up the challenge. They spotted the battalion of German infantry supporting the tanks, which had fallen behind their Mark IVs. The gunners went to work with a will. They slaughtered the German 'stubble-hoppers', as the enemy infantry called themselves, without mercy.

> There is a really strange feeling to be standing here. Five tanks have broken through. Four had already been hit when the fifth was coming by me. I was behind this tree. Right after it passed, I stepped out and let him have it with the bazooka. It went a few more yards, then went off the road up there where you see that bale of hay. The Germans came tearing out of that tank, let me tell you. They were ready to fight. We shot them down.
>
> SGT. JACKSON OF THE 502ND PARACHUTE INFANTRY TO THE REPORTER OF THE 'STARS AND STRIPES'

That cold unfeeling prose shows just how much the ice of battle had entered the hearts of the fighting men on both sides of the line that day. It was Christmas Day all right, but the Lord both foe and friend worshipped was seemingly looking the other way ...

Despite the new German attacks on Bastogne, it was clear to Kokott of the 26th People's Grenadier Division, who had carried the main burden of the assault ever since 18th December, that they were making no real headway; the 'Amis' were simply too strong. On the morning of 26th December, Kokott was informed that there were twelve

American tanks at Assensois not far from his command post, 'firing in all directions'.

> We tried to get reinforcements there [to Heilmann's paras to the south of Bastogne] but the troops of my 26th Volksgrenadier Division were so exhausted from the fighting that they simply couldn't make the effort. They had simply run out of strength and courage. I knew it was all over.
>
> GENERAL KOKOTT TO HIS US INTERROGATORS AFTER THE WAR

Kokott was right. Perhaps if the People's Grenadiers had acted more assertively that day the course of the Battle of Bastogne might have been different. Remnants of a whole Panzer Korps from the stalled 6th SS Panzer Army were already on their way to the 5th Army front. But the die had already been cast.

Under the command of America's future top general in Vietnam, Creighton Abrams, in 1944 a colonel in the Fourth Armored Division, the final four-mile dash for Bastogne had begun on the afternoon of 26th December 1944. Patton was breathing down Abrams' neck hard and the latter knew he had to make it this day - or else.

In the lead Sherman was a thirty-three year old veteran, Lt. Charles Boggess. Years later when Boggess returned to the scene of his triumph, bald, tubby and small, and looking very mild mannered, no one thought that he had once been the hero of the hour. But he was. Now under the cover of a concentrated artillery bombardment on Assensois, he and his column broke loose. They started to push into what was the virtual unknown; 'Indian country', as they called it in those far-off days.

Desperately the last survivors of Heilmann's decimated Fifth Para Division tried to stop the Amis. To no avail! Nothing dare hold up Boggess and his little column of vulnerable Shermans though it only needed a determined German boy armed with a panzerfaust to put him out of action in a flash. Behind them rattled the White half-tracks, packed with the Fourth's armoured infantrymen. The paras reeled back. Here and there when the column ground to a half, the American infantry dropped from their vehicles and took the young German fanatics on, hand-to-hand. Now no quarter was given or expected. All the same, Boggess was taking serious casualties. Within sight of the beleaguered Belgian township, he was down to his last tank, two others from his Company C of the 37th Tank Battalion, and a couple of half-tracks.

Now it was getting dark. Still no sign of the 101st Airborne perimeter. With the barrel of his 75 mm cannon still glowing from the twenty-off shells the gun fired in Assensois and later, Boggess pressed on ever deeper into 'Indian Country'. About four thirty that December afternoon, just after one of his remaining half-tracks had been knocked out, the tubby Captain spotted a small green-painted bunker. Beyond coloured red and white parachutes hung in the trees and lay abandoned in the enemy fields. They didn't concern a worried Boggess. He knew he was way out on a limb. As soon as darkness fell completely, he would be easy meat for any young Kraut fanatic.

Being very careful now, he ordered his corporal gunner to let the supposed bunker have a couple of rounds. The gunner, also well aware of their tricky situation, did so with alacrity. The solid shot armour-piercing shell whizzed visibly through the air and slammed into the concrete (the mark is still there). He followed it up with a couple of rounds of H.E. (high explosive). That did it. Scores of shadowy figures fled into the trees.

Boggess felt he had made it. He didn't know why, he just sensed it in his bones. Carefully he opened the turret hatch and called, "Come here! This is the Fourth Armored".

A soldier - he couldn't make out whether friend or foe in the growing gloom - approached him slowly, carbine cradled in his arms. Suddenly the unknown soldier beamed all over his face. He called back, 'Lieutenant Duane J. Webster... 326th Engineer Battalion 101st Airborne'. The ring around Bastogne had been broken!

To the Germans the Team of Abrams and Cohen seems like the instrument of a wrathful Jehovah.

LIFE MAGAZINE, 1945[24]

The breaking of the siege did not result only in the receipt of supplies and much needed reinforcements, it also brought in the first newspapers since mid-December. Suddenly the 'Eagles' discovered they were national heroes. As the 101st's first divisional history of 1945 put it: 'they had become a legend... ten thousand daily maps [were] showing one spot holding out inside the rolling tide of the worst American military debacle of modern times'.

That four-letter answer - 'Nuts!' - to the German demand for surrender helped mightily. Patton naturally did all he could to make the most of his victory before the massive Allied counter-attack, which would be under the secret command of the 'Limey Fart', Montgomery, commenced. And although the Battle of Bastogne would continue right into the New Year, the 'visiting firemen', plus the representatives of press and radio, descended upon the weary, slightly bemused survivors. They were not the only ones.

General Taylor, who had been on leave or reporting to higher command in Washington (depending on what was your opinion of the handsome, clever paratroop commander), managed finally to get through to his battered division. It seemed that his return was not altogether welcomed by the rank-and-file. There appeared to be a feeling that he had deserted the 'Eagles', that he had never really possessed any deep regard for the Division which he hadn't created and whose commander he had become by chance.

He [Taylor] inspected the front lines very briskly. His instructions before leaving us were 'watch those woods in front of you'. What the hell did he think we had been doing while he was in Washington?

RICHARD WINTERS, 101ST AB

Indeed although the 'Eagles' were naturally proud to be the heroes of the day, they definitely took an intense dislike to those who tried to steal some of their newfound glory. Even McAuliffe (who had been criticized himself by the 101st on account of that Christmas Eve picture in the cellar and the makeshift Christmas tree and who would soon be given a division of his own due to his performance in Bastogne), felt constrained to have a go at the visiting firemen, battlefield tourists and those who would try to steal the 101st's victory at the Belgian city.

Naturally Patton and his Third Army was one of the prime targets for his dislike of the new 'Bastogne Legend'. Patton being Patton had swiftly made his appearance in the town which he had originally wanted abandoning. He had been photographed shaking hands with McAuliffe, presenting him with a medal and going through one of his customary performances for the benefit of the media. No one made as good a copy as 'Old Blood an' Guts'. That's why the Press liked him so much.

McAuliffe didn't.

The 101st Airborne call themselves the triple 'B's. Battered Bastards of Bastogne. They did well, but like the Marines of the last war, they got more credit than they deserve.

GEN. PATTON, JANUARY 1945

From now onwards till the day he died, McAuliffe would maintain stoutly and defiantly that Bastogne had never been surrounded, and even if it had been, there had been no need of a 'rescue attempt'. Indeed as he told the reporters at the time in a statement that made the headlines back in the States: *'101st AB Division General Says No 'Rescue' Took Place'*.

To keep the record straight, Brig. Gen. Anthony G. McAuliffe emphatically asserted that his 101st Airborne Div. was not rescued at Bastogne. 'Anyone who says we were rescued or thinks we needed rescue is all wrong. On Christmas night I called my regimental commanders together and told them we were now ready for the pursuit'.

MCAULIFFE TO THE STARS AND STRIPES, SATURDAY 6TH JAN. 1945

Be that as it may, all that McAuliffe's weary and, in some cases, disillusioned paratroopers knew that last week of December was that they were not going to be withdrawn from the line to lick their wounds and enjoy a desperately needed rest. General Patton needed 'bodies' - they were going to be those bodies! They'd have to fight on.

VII

OPERATION NORTHWIND

Just before midnight on the last day of the old year, Sunday 31st December 1944, two young American officers decided that someone ought to celebrate the 'Year of Victory', 1945. Lieutenants George Bradshaw and Richard Shattuck clambered out of their foxholes in Fox Company's front line and despite the freezing cold started to count off the minutes to the New Year.

For nearly two days now the relatively green 44th Infantry Division, to which they belonged, had been dug in between the French industrial towns of Sarreguemines and Rimling. Here their division was at the extreme left of the US Seventh Army's long line in the Saar-Alsace[25] area close to the Siegfried Line and Germany.

Here though the fighting still raged in the 'Bulge', in particular around the newly relieved Bastogne, it had been mostly quiet. There had been occasional artillery duels, reports of spies, a minor flap or two. But even the greenhorns from the 44th knew from the anxious looks on the German-speaking local French that, to use the crude phrase of the time, 'the crap was soon gonna hit the fan'. The question remained - where?

During New Year's Eve day there had been several minor disturbances in front of the snowbound Fox Company. The best of them had been when five company booby traps had gone off delivering to the tense GIs not dead Germans, but dead rabbits, which were hurriedly cut up and provided a welcome change from C rations.

Now unabashed by the knowledge that something unpleasant as in the air, the two young officers stood in the moonlit snow, while the men watched keeping their thoughts about the madness of temporary officers and gentlemen to themselves, carbine raised now to fire a pagan 'feu de joie' to welcome the New Year.

"Two minutes to go", Bradshaw called to Shattuck. He clicked off his safety catch and watched the second hand of the green-glowing dial of his wristwatch. Shattuck did the same. The countdown commenced.

But Bradshaw and his old friend were not fated to fire the salute of welcome to the New Year. Suddenly, surprisingly, their ears were deafened by a great roar. Next moment gull bullets started kicking up the snow all around Shattuck in vicious sprays of white. That instant a fighter plane dropped out of the velvet, star-studded night sky. It came in at zero feet. Behind it, it dragged its monstrous black shadow across the snowfield. Violent flames rippled the length of the Messer-

95

schmitt's wings. Slugs beat up the positions of the confused, frightened Fox Company men everywhere. A second later it was gone, as suddenly as it had appeared, roaring up into the night sky in a tight curve, leaving behind it a loud echoing silence that seemed to reverberate around the surrounding hills for ever.

Shakily Shattuck rose to his feet, patting the snow from his uniform. Behind his men poked their ashen, unshaven faces over the rims of their foxholes. In an awed voice, Bradshaw called to his buddy: "What the hell's going on, Dick?"

Shattuck shook his head, not able to speak. But already he could hear the rusty rattle of tank tracks to Fox's Company front, and he didn't need a crystal ball to know what that meant. There were no American tanks out there. It was the Krauts. The long-expected German attack was on its way.

Our people are resolved to fight the war to victory under any and all circumstances... We are going to destroy everybody who does not take part in the effort for the country or makes himself a tool of the enemy... The world must know that this State will never capitulate... Germany will rise like a phoenix from its ruined cities and will go down in history as the miracle of the 20th century! I want, therefore, in this hour, as spokesman of Greater Germany, to promise solemnly to the Almighty that we shall fulfil our duty faithfully and unshakably in the New Year, in the firm belief that the hour will strike when victory will ultimately come to him who is most worthy of it, the Greater German Reich!
ADOLF HITLER, MIDNIGHT 31ST DEC. 1944, RADIO BERLIN

The German counter-attack in the West – 'Operation Northwind' had commenced ...

On that midnight, the survivors of the 101st Airborne in Bastogne an area had been engaged in operations against the increasingly heavy German attacks for five days now.

They had believed on 26th December, the day that Patton had broken through with his Fourth Armored Division, that would be withdrawn and sent back to Mourmelon-le-Grand for a well-earned rest. They had been sadly mistaken. Patton had instead incorporated them in his Third Army and kept them in the line. Indeed he had gone even further. Worn out as they were, sadly reduced in numbers, lacking vital supplies, he had thrown them into limited offensive operations against the ever-growing strength of the Germans under von Manteuffel.

The site of the 'Battle of Devizes' in 1944.
The 101st's first engagement in WWII. It was between the
British 'Red Devils' and the 'Screaming Eagles'.
Cause - women and drink!

'The Hard' at Brixham, Devon (UK) from which the
US 4th Division sailed. The ground link-up for troops sailing to
Utah Beach (4th, 90th and 101st Airborne US Divisions)

Gen. Dwight D. Eisenhower visits men of the 502nd 101st Airborne
Division at Greenham Common on 5th June 1944.

Slapton Sand (England), scene of 'Operation Tiger', today.

Maj. Gen. Maxwell D. Taylor
receiving the
Distinguished Service Cross
from Gen. Montgomery.

Gen. Taylor's Command Post in Normandy, today.

99

506th PIR 101st Div
Tpr. Wilbur W.
Shanklin
with a
German prisoner.

101st Airborne casualties around St-Marie-du-Mont.

Spot where Gen. Pratt was killed 6th June, Normandy.

PRATT MEMORIAL

BEFORE DAWN JUNE 6 1944 BRIGADIER GENERAL DON F. PRATT, ASSISTANT DIVISION COMMANDER 101ST AIRBORNE DIVISION (UNITED STATES ARMY) WAS KILLED WHEN HIS GLIDER CRASHED 250 METRES EAST OF THIS POINT. HE WAS THE FIRST GENERAL ALLIED FORCES OFFICER KILLED IN THE LIBERATION OF FRANCE.

AVANT L'AUBE LE 6 JUIN 1944 LE GENERAL DE BRIGADE DON F. PRATT, COMMANDANT ADJOINT DE LA 101EME DIVISION AEROPORTEE DE L'ARMEE DES ETATS-UNIS A ETE TUE LORS DE L'ECRASEMENT DE SON PLANEUR A 250 METRES A L'EST DE CE LIEU. IL ETAIT LE PREMIER OFFICIER GENERAL DES FORCES ALLIEES A DONNER SA VIE POUR LA LIBERATION DE LA FRANCE.

The glider 'The Flying Falcon' in which Gen. Pratt was killed.

SS Grenadier of the German 17th SS Panzergrenadier Division
which also opposed the 101st Airborne.
Note the 'flak' bursts in the sky.

Waiting for 'Old Jerry'. The 'Red Devils' of the British 1st Airborne
in an ambush position.

Victory! for the 'Screaming Eagles'.

The cost! Normandy cemetery of the 101st Airborne.

Entering Cherbourg, the conquering hero
Gen. 'Lightning Joe' Collins
Commander VII Corps, to which 101st belonged.

The victor!
Patton's grave among the dead
of the 3rd Army
and 101st Airborne
at Hamm, Luxembourg.

Ardennes today.

Crossing point of von Luttwitz's Corps (16/17th December) today.

The start of the attack on Bastogne, River Our/Sauer line.

Fugitives from 28th Infantry Div who reached Bastogne
to take part in the siege.

'Black Watch' of British 51st Highland Division
moving in the direction of Bastogne.

US infantry in 'house-to-house' work on the other side of the Rhine.

The remains of the Remagen Bridge. The most famous bridge in the world - for a week.

Looking at the Rhine, west bank, defended by 101st/82nd Airborne. Here Cologne, its cathedral and the ruined Hohenzollern Bridge.

'Watch on the Rhine' - 'Screaming Eagle' style!

Hitler, pre-war on his daily walk to the teahouse at Berchtesgaden.

The 'Brown Eminence' -
Martin Bormann,
Hitler's secretary,
who built the
mountain retreat.

Hermann Goering
sweating it out after
his capture in the
mountains beyond
Berchtesgaden.

The original Hitler homes before the bombing by the RAF.

'Eagle's Nest' - Berchtesgaden.

The exit of the mysterious 'Bormann tunnel' today.
All that survives of the labours of the 'Brown Eminence'.

Hatfield, England.
Here in WWII the famed RAF wooden bomber, the 'Mosquito' was
built. In our time, Steven Spielberg had his backdrop villages for
Private Ryan and *Band of Brothers* built here.

Montgomery's British XXX Corps had ensured that his Fifth Army would be unable to cross the Meuse and carry out the Führer's grandiose plan for a drive to Brussels and Antwerp. So the little ex-gentleman jockey Manteuffel was settling for what the German General Staff called the 'smaller solution' in the Ardennes; holding on to territory west of Germany's frontier. With the recapture of this territory and the great losses inflicted on the Americans, this could still be regarded as a victory. It might well give Germany vitally needed time and certainly it would ensure that the Allied timetable for the attack on the Reich itself would be put back at least a month.

Patton, however, did not intend to give von Manteuffel a chance to recover. The former's aims were not merely strategic however. He wanted to achieve some sort of major victory with the forces at his disposal, before the US 1st Army to the north of the Bulge and the British XXX Corps to the south-west cracked into action in a massive attack which would certainly defeat von Manteuffel. Patton's haste to attack was, in part, to beat that combined attack; for it would be led by Montgomery. And Montgomery was not going to get kudos of victory in the Bulge. After all, it had been quite truly, virtually an all-American battle and it would be won, in Patton's opinion, by American troops led by American generals, in particular naturally, *General George S. Patton*. Besides, after initial defeat in the Bulge, America needed heroes - and Patton intended to be that hero.

Patton's manoeuvring of Third Army to relieve Bastogne did not win the Battle of the Bulge. Indeed as historians have pointed out, the relief of Bastogne was made in a sector occupied by inferior German formations and the heaviest attacks on Bastogne did not commence until December 26... If the entire Ardennes campaign resembled a Wagnerian melodrama... it was for Patton a western film: like the cavalry of yore to the rescue of homesteaders in a dramatic cliff-hanger, culminating with Third Army in the role of cavalry and Patton at its head, rallying his troops.
LT. COL. CARLO D'ESTE, US ARMY RETD. 'A GENIUS FOR WAR'

Naturally the 'homesteaders' in the form of 'Eagles' of the battered 101st Airborne Division didn't like it one bit. Instead of enjoying the fruits of their victory which had made them heroes back home, they were going into action once more with such greenhorns as the troopers of the 17th Airborne Division, rushed over from the UK to help stem the German tide of aggression. Why? They told themselves scornfully, 'Not even the commanding general, Miley, had ever heard a shot fired in anger'.[26]

The 'Eagles' blamed firstly Patton and then their own regimental commanders and the Division's other top brass, in particular the 'leave man', General Taylor. Their own senior officers, they felt, should have stood up to Patton and saved them from further combat. Now here they were, stating that the 101st had never been in any real trouble in Bastogne and they were ready to have another go at the 'Krauts'.

> When the word came down for this attack [on the village of Noville just outside Bastogne] it pissed me off. I could not believe that after what we had gone through and done, after all the casualties we had suffered, they were putting us into the attack. It just had the flavour of an ego trip for General Taylor, a play to show Eisenhower that now Taylor's back, his troops will get off their arses and go into the attack.
>
> CAPTAIN WINTERS, 101ST AB

The 101st's rank-and-file, it appeared, were becoming 'bolshy'. To some extent they had good reason to be anti-establishment. Admittedly they were facing enemy decisions such as the 12th SS Panzer, 'The Hitler Youth', which had been badly mauled further north. But the young fanatics of the SS, who suffered 10,000 casualties in Normandy, including all their battalion, regimental and one divisional commander, were the best the Wehrmacht possessed in the winter of '44/45. They knew their beloved Führer had ordered that the front at Bastogne should be held; they were determined to carry out that order, cost what it may.

But they hadn't reckoned with the men of the 'Screaming Eagle Division'. They were equally tough and as 'bolshy' as they were, they still carried out their orders and carried out their attacks with the same verve that they had done in Normandy and Holland. The assault on Noville, which Captain Winters thought was General Taylor's ploy to please Eisenhower, was typical. Although it had been one of the 101st's objectives since 20th December 1944, nearly a month before, the Division had never achieved its aim. Now they did so, believing their own lies, as it were, that this would be the last place they'd be called upon to attack before they were sent back for a rest! But the 'Eagles' would be in for an unpleasant surprise; it wasn't.

The going was tough. It was not that the enemy infantry, mostly SS, was supported by the great lumbering Panthers of the most senior SS Division, Die Leibstandarte, Adolf Hitler (The Adolf Hitler Bodyguard Division), but the weather also seemed to conspire to stop the progress of the attackers. Unlike the Germans, used to the war in Russia, the Americans had no special greases and oils to stop their vehicles and equipment from seizing up. Nor were they provided with their clothing or food that the Germans enjoyed. The 'Eagles' might have possessed lemonade powder in their canned rations (very useful in sub-arctic temperatures), but the Germans had bricks of concentrated pea soup. This thrown into a can of boiling water would provide a meal of nourishing, rib-filling soup, tasting of smoked sausage, however ersatz, which the German doughboy called - truthfully - 'fart soup'. Even the German boots, worn packed with straw and one size too large, together with foot rags rather than socks (which caused blisters), were better than the endemic frostbite and trenchfoot of the US Army.

Still the 'Eagles' pushed forward bravely, fighting the weather at the same time that they pushed the Germans out of their well-established positions. Often the fighting deteriorated into a bloody, savage hand-to-hand scrap when knives and sharpened spades were used brutally instead of firearms. In the case of Sergeant Hale, for example, he managed to shoot an SS officer just after the latter had slashed the American's throat with his knife.

Bleeding heavily and obviously dying, Hale was rushed on the bonnet of a jeep down to the US medical hospital in Luxembourg. Here the sweating hard-pressed medics managed to patch him, leaving the NCO with a crooked oesophagus. Upon recovering, Hale was told by a doctor that he did not need to wear a necktie. Later Patton encountered the Sergeant, who seemingly had committed one of the most heinous crimes in the Third Army's commander's book. He was improperly dressed! But before 'Old Blood an' Guts' could fine the criminal on the spot, Sergeant Hale triumphantly produced the doctors' 'pink slip' indicating that the medic has excused him from wearing a necktie while in the services. Patton's comments are not recorded, but it doesn't require a great brain to imagine them!

For another couple of days the attack went on, heading for Houfflaize where the US 1st and 3rd Armies would finally cut off the Bulge, bringing the Battle to an official end (though pockets of Germans held out everywhere). Out of defeat, victory had been finally snatched - at a cost.

The 101st's role at Bastogne was over at last. What now?

Well, Jesus Christ, if it isn't O'Farrell. I didn't recognise you in a tank. I haven't seen you since Fort Fox.
EXCHANGE BETWEEN COL. O'FARRELL AND COL. FOY AT THE OFFICIAL LINK OF THE 1ST AND 3RD US ARMIES AT HOUFFLAIZE, JANUARY 1945

It was certain even now that they were not going back for a rest. Patton had used them for his purpose. Now with infantrymen in short supply all along Eisenhower's tremendously long front running from the Swiss border at Southern Holland, they were going to be moved to another section, again to be used as 'doughs', ordinary infantry. It was almost as if they were those 18th century Hessians, whose Dukes had sold to the highest bidder and had met their final defeat at the hands of those 'colonialists' who rebelled against King George of England. Now with Patton finishing with their services, they were on their way, transferred to the next highest bidder, namely General 'Sandy' Patch, commander of the US 7th Army in the Saar-Alsace ...

"It must have been hell", said one of the glider pilots. "It sure must have been hell." Entangled with the branches of a tree, a human leg dangled. On the adjacent slope a man had slowly frozen as his life ebbed away and all around him were the bodies of other Germans who had died in a charge down the slope... It was bitterly cold, the air sharp with frost. When night fell, the vehicles were on the wider, smoother paving of a main road and sped rapidly southwards. A bright moon rose over the dark forests and shone down brilliantly on the freezing dejected soldiers in the open trucks ...

REPORTER FRED MACKENZIE, RECORDING THE DEPARTURE OF THE SURVIVORS OF THE 101ST FROM BASTOGNE

By the time the survivors of the 101st Airborne had begun to take part in the forgotten 'Second Battle of the Bulge', General Alexander 'Sandy' Patch's Seventh Army had been fighting the Germans in the Saar-Alsace region for nearly three weeks. Unlike the soldiers of the original 'Bulge', they had not been taken by surprise. The British secret de-coding operation at 'Station X' (Bletchley Park) had warned them that the Germans would attack once Patton had made his move north.

Indeed at that celebrated Verdun conference on 19th December when Patton had been ordered into the counter-attacking, Eisenhower had warned General Devers,[27] whom the Supreme Commander disliked intensely, to be prepared to withdraw if the Germans attacked. It was the only time during the whole course of the European campaign that 'Ike' *ordered* an American commander to give up ground.

Now, the US 7th Army, warned as they had been, had been fighting all-out against the fierce German attack and suffering consequently. Some of the divisions involved were seasoned veterans, such as the US 45th and 3rd Divisions, which had been fighting since 1943; others were total greenhorns as was the US 70th Division straight off the boat at Marseilles. But greenhorns and new boys, they had all suffered tremendous casualties. The 70th, for example, had already incurred nearly 3,000 dead, wounded, captured and missing and Patton's 'bodies' were urgently required to bolster up the Seventh Army's shaky line. Not only that, Devers had finally complied with Eisenhower's order of the previous December: he was going to shorten his line by pulling back his 6th Corps. It was something that all US commanders dreaded; to give up ground 'bought by American blood' (as General Bradley once put it). But it had to be done and it was in the midst of this confused unseeming mess that the men of the 101st started to arrive on the new battlefield in France.

There was relief, but not real relief. Behind were their friends and comrades, in rubble of towns and on those fields and more of their friends and comrades were in the hospitals... They felt a little as if they were giving up, as if they had fought and suffered and died in vain... And it was a bitter grating night, that night, of tears in the soul... and it snowed.

DIVISION HISTORY OF THE US 14TH ARMORED DIV.

Not telling the French civilians what was going on and warning them that on the morrow, the SS and Gestapo would probably be swarming through their shattered villages and townships, arresting those who had worked with the Amis. In due course, such unfortunates would be heading for the concentration camps of the Reich, for since the 1940 annexation of this part of France, the German-speaking locals had been regarded as German nationals. Instead the Americans sneaked out in a raging snowstorm like thieves in the night. Behind them the French started to follow. They knew anything was better than the return of the *Boche*.

It was cold that, a bitter cold that ate into our bones. It snowed that night, a blinding blanket that wet us to the skin. We retreated that night, a retreat that hurt our minds. But worst of all was what our eyes told our soul. Our eyes saw people, newly liberated French people, trudging back down those snowbound roads with their houses on their backs and despair in their steps. Hordes of civilians who had trusted us, moving once again to escape the imminence of a German advance.

THE HISTORIAN OF THE US 222ND INFANTRY REGIMENT

General Brooks, commanding the Seventh Army's Sixth Corps, had moved his men back to the line of the River Moder. Here on the night of 24/25th January 1945, six German divisions struck the 6th

Corps. In particular, the three thousand men of the 42nd (Rainbow) Division, standing up to their knees in snowwater in their foxholes, were hit by elements of *five* German regiments, drawn from *three* divisions, including the tanks of the 25th Panzer Division.

At six o'clock that freezing January night, the enemy artillery burst into activity. The enemy guns started to run a creeping barrage to the US positions on the river valley lines which ran between the Alsation villages of Neubourg and Schewighausen. For one long interminable hour the Germans plastered the American positions. Then as surprisingly as the barrage had commenced, it ceased.

> We waited. Sweat. THEN! All bammed and clattered, streaked and crashed around us until 20.00 hours. Shapeless blobs started to poke up out of their positions, moved around and started towards. ONRUSH! Spit on your muzzles, sweetheart, here comes the devil.
>
> HISTORY OF THE 222ND US INFANTRY REGIMENT

By morning the Sixth Corps' line was under attack everywhere and Seventh Army was sending almost panic-stricken signals to find out the positions of the 101st convoys heading south. For they were the only reinforcements immediately available. It hadn't altogether reckoned with the steadfastness of his greenhorns of the 42nd and the 14th Armored Divisions. Here and there admittedly the line was giving, but they were still holding and in the case of the 14th Armored actually counter-attacking. All the same it was nip-and-tuck and a captured SS prisoner from the 6th SS Mountain Division revealed a frightening secret to Seventh Army Intelligence: Himmler, the head of the SS, intended to recapture the Alsation capital of Strasbourg for 30th January 1945 as a surprise present for the Führer. It would be a way of celebrating the twelfth anniversary of his acceptance of power as German Chancellor on that same date in 1933. It was clear that one way or another, the 'Eagles' were urgently needed in Alsace.

> Our morale was already pretty low. I had gone into Bastogne with forty men in the platoon and there were only fourteen of us left, counting the mortar squad - and that was not an abnormally shrunken unit. We had lost a lot of people and those who were left were feeling pretty much that the war was a lousy business and that we had been ill-used and we were hardly cheering about the fact of going down and trying to pull the chestnuts out of the fire in another area.
>
> LT. SEFTON, 501ST PARACHUTE INFANTRY REGIMENT

Arriving, frozen, hungry and to some extent downhearted, on 26th January, the men of the 327th and 501st relieved the hard-hit 222nd Infantry of the Seventh Army's 6th Corps. Here along the line of the River Moder, to their flanks the veteran 79th Infantry Division and the 103rd 'Cactus' Division (named after its divisional patch), now commanded by a familiar figure: no less a person than General McAuliffe of Bastogne.

The gliderborne troops and the paras didn't like what they found there. The men of the 42nd, a famous division in WWI, had not lived up to their reputation. They had left far too many of their dead on the battlefield where they had fallen and there is nothing a combat soldier dislikes more than seeing his own dead abandoned to the elements; naturally it reminds him of just how unimportant his own death in battle would be. In the end the 'Eagles' protested and the bodies were removed. But it set a pattern.

Prior to the arrival of the 101st the Rainbow Division men had acquired a habit, obviously based on the wartime 'Kilroy was Here' fad, of painting a little rainbow on everything adorned with the legend, 'The Rainbow Division was Here'. The cynical and disgusted troopers of the 101st adapted the sign, adding to it their own contemptuous graffiti: 'Where the Hell are you now?'

But despite their limited success in Northern Alsace, the Germans had shot their bolt in the Moder River Line. Now the action was moving south to where the remains of the German 19th Army were trapped in what was called 'the Colmar Pocket', named after the major city of the area. As far as the airborne men were concerned, their combat activities with the Seventh Army's 6th Corps were limited to aggressive patrolling across the river and behind the German lines in that rugged, well-wooded area.

Not that the troopers were particularly keen to get themselves killed in this backwater of the war - in the 'Bitch Bulge', as they were calling it, perhaps already aware that post-war history would totally neglect Seventh Army's war, in particular this Second Battle of the Bulge.[28] But General Taylor was a stern taskmaster. After his absence from Bastogne, the West Pointer, who knew that promotion in the Regular Army meant being successful in battle and that World War Two wouldn't go on for ever, now had to be seen doing things. Besides, good soldier that he was, he knew his paras would go stale on him soon - very soon - if they were left, idle. Tough hard-drinking bunch that the 'Eagles' were, he well realised that the Devil should soon find work for their idle hands and that would mean the same disciplinary problems he had faced with his men after the return to France from the drop in Holland back in the Fall. So Taylor reasoned, if the Krauts wouldn't come to him, he'd have to go to them. This meant small scale attacks across the River Moder.

Thus it was that the two parachute regiments would take turns in platoon and company-sized assaults across the fast-flowing mountain river. The usual reasons were given by the Brass for these patrols - reconnaissance, intelligence, wanted prisoners, new men had to be 'bloodied', etc. etc. And although the veterans didn't like it, there were always adventure foolish kids, or young officers straight from the Point, ready for some 'desperate glory', eager to volunteer.

Some such as Lt. Hugo Sims, commanding A Company of the 501st, was so eager that he crossed the Moder at the double, even though he and his more reluctant troopers were well behind the enemy lines. Indeed his radioman, Ed Hallo, had to run up to the young captain and tell him, 'Captain, slow down. You're losing your men back there'.

> He [Sims] didn't know the men in the company and he had given orders that if anybody got wounded they had to make it back on their own - don't stop to help anyone hit... So we went up there, we got along a road and those Germans came up in platoons formation. 'Links... links... links...' When they got in the middle of us we let loose and we slaughtered them.
>
> ED HALLO, 101ST AB

The radio operator with the apt name might not have showed such compassion: 'we slaughtered them'. But the veterans had become like that, ruthless killing machines. All the same, he and his fellow 'old heads' didn't much like officers who seemed to them to be glory-hunters. Sims got his Silver Star for the action, but that didn't win him much respect among the men he had led, even though he praised them, in particular Hallo.

> He [Sims] turned to me and said, "Hallo, this won't get you the Silver Star, but I don't know what I would've done without you". I didn't say anything and you could've heard a pin drop. This guy, every time you turned around, he got a medal.
>
> E. HALLO

Casualties from these raids were low by Airborne standards. It was fortunate. For there were great gaps in the 'Eagles' ranks still from the Bulge and they were steadily absorbing replacements, who looked up in awe at the veterans. As for the latter, they felt they had won the right to look like those two famous *Stars and Stripes* cartoon characters, who were the bane of many a senior officer's life, including Patton's - Willie and Joe.

These vets felt they had a right to go around incorrectly dressed, carrying more captured German weapons, in particular the German Schmeisser machine pistol, than American ones, unshaven and, in some cases, apparently unwashed. As the Duke of Wellington had expressed it a century before when regarding his own ragtail army, 'I don't know if they frighten the Frenchies, but they damn well frighten me, sir!' They certainly frightened the new boys straight from the States.

None of them talked much; they all looked extremely exhausted and they were all absolutely filthy dirty - every inch of their uniforms. Apparently, in Bastogne, they'd never had much chance to change or wash or do anything except eat and survive.
NEW REPLACEMENT, KEN PARKER, 506TH PARACHUTE INFANTRY

In secret, they kept to themselves, the veterans were scared by the arrival of these callow teenage replacements while the Division was still in the front line. It could mean only one thing, they told themselves. They were being built up for another operational jump. As Captain Webster put it angrily after the war, recalling the arrival of 'four very scared, very young boys fresh from jump school. Why did the Army with all its mature huskies in rear echelon and the Air Corps alone in England choose to send its youngest, most inexperienced members straight from basic training to the nastiest job in the world, front line infantry?'

It was the age-old complaint of all armies, especially the American in WWII, where they invariably complained about the way it was run in battle - 'one man in the line and five to bring up the coca-cola!'

Teach 'em to say 'Follow me' and ship them overseas was the quickest way to replace casualties.
HANK JONES, REPLACEMENT FROM WEST POINT TO THE 101ST, FEBRUARY 1945

In February 1945 Webster and the rest of the 'old heads' were right: the 'Eagles' *were* being built up for a new jump and the divisional commander, Taylor, plus his fellow airborne generals were falling over each other to get into airborne combat once more before the war in Europe ended.

For now there was a whole airborne corps, the 18th, commanded by the senior airborne general, Ridgway, who had first gone into combat in Sicily in July 1943 and had been instrumental in helping to save the fledgling airborne divisions from being broken up. Under his command on the Continent he had the 101st, the 82nd and the new 17th Airborne Division, which had suffered greatly as infantry in the Bulge but which had still to make its first combat jump. In the UK, he had the two veteran British airborne divisions, the 6th AB and the 1st AB, which was being reformed after the debacle at Arnhem, plus the US 13th Airborne, still in training (and which was destined to be the only US airborne formation in Europe in WWII not too make a combat jump). This great force was being prepared for something - those at the top knew that. They guessed that once the Rhine had been crossed, there could be only one German objective worthy of significant airborne losses: the Home of the Beast, Berlin and Hitler's Bunker!

Such significant matters naturally didn't concern the lowly troopers. They were pre-occupied with the basics of a fighting infantryman's existence, as brutal, mean and often dramatically short, as it was: staying alive, finding a shelter and with a bit of luck, a bottle of hooch and some fresh meat instead of lemonade powder and canned pork - 'armored pig' - that came up with the rations with monotonous regularity.

They went on patrols, took a delight in destroying Germans and German military property, and bitched about the civilians back home who hadn't an idea in hell about the kind of lives they lived out here in the front line in this remote part of France, which most 'civvies' wouldn't be able to find on a map. As Captain, soon to be Major, Webster wrote to his parents after the death of one of his young soldiers during a patrol, how the 'kid' had shrieked and moaned when he had been hit on a patrol by Webster's company. 'He wasn't twenty years old... he hadn't begun to live. But now he was crying out in his extreme pain for his comrades carrying him back to kill him.'

He [the 'kid] gave up his life on a stretcher. Back in America the standard living continued to rise. Back in America the racetracks were booming, the nightclubs were making their greatest profits in history. Miami Beach was so crowded you couldn't get a room anywhere. Few people seemed to care. Hell, this was a boom, this was prosperity, this was the way to fight a war... We wondered if the people would ever know that it costs soldiers in terror, bloodshed and hideous, agonizing deaths to win the war.

CAPTAIN WEBSTER

It had always been thus. The people back home had never real-ised what the man in line goes through. How could they? Perhaps it was better, especially for mothers, wives, girlfriends, that they never *should* know.

But as March approached that final spring of the war in Europe, the 101st's sojourn in the Alsace area was beginning to come to an end. On 23rd February the 101st was relieved by the veteran 36 (Texas) Division, which had been fighting since 1943 and had - rightly so[29] - a grudge against the Top Brass itself. There were parades. For a hand-ful of very lucky veterans, there was a furlough to the States. They returned to Mourmelon for a second time, again in a different Division than the one that had first gone to the French barracks complex, in what now seemed another age.

The Supreme Commander came to inspect the cleaned up 'Ea-gles' personally. The brass was paraded in front of him, spick-and-span in their Class A uniforms, complete with badges, ribbons, for-eign decorations - the works. Eisenhower, together with Ridgway, was introduced to Sergeant Hale, the only man in the whole European Theatre of Operations excused from wearing a necktie. That informa-tion pleased 'Ike'. He shook Hale's hand and gave his speech - divi-sional brass always expected speeches from their senior command-ers.

> You were given a marvellous opportunity [at Bastogne] and you met every test... I'm awfully proud of you.
> GEN. EISENHOWER, 10TH MARCH 1945

For a commander, who only four months before had been pre-pared to hang the naughty boys among the 'Screaming Eagles' at Rheims to appease the outraged French, it was an amazing 'volte face'. So they left France for the unknown. The war still had three bloody months to run. What would it hold for the 101st Airborne Division? Many of its senior officers, as we have seen, though they knew. But the one man at the March parade who really knew the 101st's final objective was playing that bloody game of poker, which is war, with his cards held tightly to his chest. The 'Eagles' were in for a surprise...

VIII

Rat Race

On Monday 2nd April 1945, *Time* magazine featured on its front cover the US general, who it proclaimed was the 'World's No. I Active Airborne Commander'. It was the first time in five years since the foundation of the US Parachute Infantry Regiment that one of its members had been portrayed on the front of America's most important news magazines.

The General *Time* honoured that day was the head of the five-month-old Allied XVIII Airborne Corps, Matthew Ridgway, and he certainly lived up to most of the magazine's rhetoric. He had been the first airborne commander to take part in combat in Sicily in 1943 and he had been in the thick of the action ever since. 'Iron Tits', as we have seen he was nicknamed by his troops on account of the grenades he carried on the lapels of his combat jacket (he carried a Springfield rifle at all times too) had struck it big.

Only a week before the *Time* cover story appeared, he had been in action with his new corps now based on the Rhine. He had killed one German personally just before another of the enemy had thrown a grenade at him. Fortunately the grenade had merely wrecked his jeep. 'By the grace of God,' he wrote later, 'the wheel was between me and the blast and all I got was one small chunk that hit me in the shoulder'.

For that brush with the enemy, General Ridgway received the 'Purple Heart' and a letter from no less than the Supreme Commander, who wrote: 'Someone told me that you were slightly wounded. Thank God it wasn't serious'.

But on that Monday when the *Time* feature appeared, things appeared to go wrong for the airborne corps commander. His three American airborne divisions, the 101st, 82nd and 17th were taken away from him. The 17th Airborne had dropped over the Rhine under Montgomery's command, while his two veteran divisions, his own old 82nd and 101st, were dug-in in a static position on the left bank of the Rhine between Bonn and Dusseldorf. Ridgway, for his part, was being given command of a new formation, made up of two infantry divisions and the experienced Seventh Armored (its commanders didn't like Ridgway: they though the hook-nosed airborne general would have sacrificed them during the Bulge if Montgomery hadn't overruled Ridgway's decision to have the surrounded Seventh stand fast). In due course this new formation would be sent north to the River Elbe to help Montgomery beat the Russians to the Baltic.

So what was to happen to Gavin's 82nd and Taylor's 101st dug-in in their static position, while another sixteen US divisions surrounded what was left of the German Army Command B in the industrial Ruhr area. What was going to be the future role of the two most elite divisions of Ridgway's airborne corps, with Ridgway departed and a new and pretty hard taskmaster in temporary charge, General 'Gravel Mouth' Harmon, an old-time armored commander?

Thirty-eight year old handsome General 'Gentleman Jim' Gavin, reputedly the lover of Marlene Dietrich,[30] had already incurred the World War One veteran's wrath by sending a whole battalion of airborne troops across the Rhine between Cologne and Bonn. There had been casualties and Harmon didn't like it.

A day or so later the commander of the 82nd Airborne, a very young major general, named James Gavin, telephoned me to report he had sent a battalion across the river [the Rhine]. The battalion had encountered so little resistance, he said, that he planned to follow it up with a regiment that night. "What did I tell you about limiting your crossing forces to platoon size?" I asked with considerable irritation. Gavin blustered a bit at first, arguing that the opposition was so slight that his entire division should be permitted to cross the Rhine.

GENERAL E. HARMON

But as Harmon told Gavin firmly that 'though the hazards might be slight there was no strategic advantage to his division's advance; there was nothing of value to us in the immediate area he proposed to move into'.

Harmon was right, of course, but he didn't say that the whole Ruhr encirclement operation, caging in nearly half a million German troops, was purposeless. What Gavin, who was much smarter than the old fire-eater knew, was there was only one strategic target left of any importance to the American troops in Germany. The capture of Berlin. Gavin knew that under the terms of the supposed top-secret 'Operation Eclipse'[31] there was still room for a sudden two division airborne drop on Berlin before the Russians took over there.

Indeed that run-in with 'Gravel Voice' encouraged an impatient Gavin, a man going somewhere. (He would become an American ambassador before he finally retired). For as he wrote later, Harmon had ordered me to 'incur no casualties in the 82nd since there was still an airborne assault envisioned'. The words were very welcome. As Gavin stated, 'airborne assault' had a particular meaning to me. They [the two words] could mean only the airborne capture of Berlin'. In the event Gavin was wrong. But appeased a little, he went back to commanding 'patrol level' activities and ensured that his highly sexed airborne division didn't break Eisenhower's new non-fraternization too openly. For as General Patton would snort later in a statement with which the airborne commander agreed: 'A man who won't fuck, won't fight... So long as my men keep their knees off the ground and their helmets on, it ain't fraternization, it's fornication'.[32]

Thus while their commanders champed at the bit, the men of the two airborne divisions dug in along the Rhine enjoyed their time out of war, resting and refitting, fraternizing if they could get away with it, definitely enjoying the fruits of abandoned German cellars, in the form of good Rhenish wine and generally living for the day.

Here and there they went across the Rhine on reconnaissance patrols. Neither the men nor their company officers took them very seriously, they were mostly interruptions in the daily routine. But sometimes, as small as these cross-Rhine patrols were, they went badly wrong for the handful of men concerned.

After dinner on 11th of April we went back to your quarters, with much laughter and horsing around, blackened our faces for the raid. In the midst of this someone bumped Santillan's mandolin from the windowsill and it smashed on the pavement below. Although it could have been an omen of things to come, no one took it as such.

PFC D. STRAITH, 506 P.I.

But it was.

Suddenly with only a fraction of a second warning, a salvo of shells bracketed our position, landing in the fields on either side and showering us with dirt.

D. STRAIT, 506TH

The Germans had spotted a little patrol and now their guns zeroed in on them. They started taking casualties. Santillan, whose mandolin had been broken, was blown in half and others wounded. By the time the patrol's boats had reached the western bank the patrol had lost three men killed in action, eleven wounded and missing. Even the three German prisoners they had taken had vanished. It wasn't a great tragedy. Nobody won a medal. No notice of the event was taken back in the States and Intelligence went without a prisoner that it didn't need anyway. But again good men died, with the war only four more short weeks to run. If the Brass still sought glory on the battlefield, the rank-and-file were sick of it. The butcher's bill paid with <u>their</u> blood was simply too high.

Even the junior officers had had enough. A replacement officer took a patrol across the Rhine, encountered fire from a single rifleman and promptly turned back to report to headquarters that he had 'met stiff resistance'. His attitude was typical. But now the 101st's time on the Rhine was coming to an end. On 18th April, all resistance from Field Marshal Model's Army Group B ended. The Field Marshal released as many of his men as possible, together with correct documentation, and went off to commit suicide - 'A German field marshal does not surrender'.[33] 325,000 German soldiers and a dozen generals, including Bayerlein and von Luettwitz of Bastogne, went into the bag. Four days later the 'Eagles' set off for what most of them was the unknown ...

The GIs called it the 'rat race'; the Germans the 'Stunde Null' (zero hour). It was a time without precedence. A chase without parallel. One of the world's most civilised, most industrialised countries had broken down completely. There was no gas, no electricity, precious little water. There was no public transport, no mail. The telephone didn't work and what radio did was mostly under Allied control. A handful of Allied Broadsheets appeared - and they were all censored. Whole cities had been wiped off the map.

Over three and a half million Germans had been killed with the Wehrmacht; another half million civilians had been killed in the air raids and fighting. There were two million cripples and currently the same number of Germans fleeing westwards in front of the advancing Russians. Ten million 'displaced persons' - everything from Czechs to Croats - moving back and forth across the shattered Reich. Mostly they simply lived off their wits, looting, stealing, raping, trying to make up their minds what to do next, taking their revenge on the Germans who had brought them here in the first place.

Naturally the black market thrived. The GI and his cigarettes, however ugly and stupid the individual soldier was, were kings. With a pack of 'Luckies' going for ten dollars and a Hershey bar for half that, the GI could have about any woman he fancied.

Don't get chummy with Jerry. In heart, body and spirit every German is a Hitler.

STARS AND STRIPES, MAY 1945

And it wasn't only their cigarettes and chocolate which brought the 'Frauleins' favours. Their men were mainly dead, maimed or prisoners. They flung themselves into the arms of these young, healthy, happy victors with a kind of joyful, despairing abandonment.[34]

What a set-up! Like a castle. Had dinner with him. What an intelligent girl friend... Cook, maid, housekeeper and secretary together with the confiscated white Mercedes - all cost him ten dollars a month.

Anon. friend on S/Sgt. Henry Kissinger's set-up in Bensheim, Hesse in 1945

Not that the men of the 101st had much opportunity to enjoy such permanent relationships as that of the future US Secretary of State that April. They were on the move now. They enjoyed being kind of tourists in uniform, but the going was rough. Everywhere the roads were out, the bridges blown, the big towns virtually impassable (soon Eisenhower in his new HQ in Frankfurt would have to issue street maps for visitors, detailing the new roads that the US Engineers had bulldozed through the ruins to the IG Farben Buildings, his headquarters). In the end the happy troopers of the 101st on their way to the unknown had to use railways, trucks and finally 'Ducks'[35], the great amphibious vehicles which had been used to cross the Rhine the previous month, to complete their journey - and incidentally, pass through four countries in the process.

It was another time out of war: one which the troopers enjoyed, especially now with the war only days to run and no prospect of their having to make another combat jump - the Russians were already surrounding Berlin with the Führer trapped inside the German capital in his bunker. They sang dirty songs, whistled at the 'Frauleins' and stripped to the waist enjoyed the spring sunshine, browning their pale, battle-scarred skinny bodies. Above all they thought of home and warmed themselves inside with the thought they'd soon be finished with the Army; the killing was almost over.

And this is number one and I've got her on the run,
Roll me over in the clover and do it agen.
Roll me over, roll me over... and do it agen.'

Popular dirty ditty of that Spring

They admired the scenery of Southern Germany, the old medieval towns such as Heidelberg, which had been spared bombing and artillery bombardments because they were hospital towns, officially declared 'open cities'. They liked the cleanliness of the Germans and their eagerness to please. Why, some of them were even volunteering to join the US Army and fight shoulder-to-shoulder with the 'Amis' against the common enemy, the Russians (or 'Ivans' as the Germans called the Americans' Russian Allies). And they swore, 'Fer Chrissake, it's a pity to waste Germany on the Krauts!'

Naturally wherever they stopped, the men looted (and not only the men, be it noted. Some of the highest-ranking generals in the Army stole art treasures, Mercedes automobiles, priceless books and the like. In some cases, as the author writes nearly sixty years later, some of this loot is being re-discovered 'at a price'!). In many cases, they stole silly things - pistols, German policemen's helmets, Nazi Party emblems and the like. Later the 101st had the pick of the defeated Reich's treasures in their possession, more spectacular items disappeared only to reappear in the States, courtesy of the US postal authorities, who weren't asking too many questions.

But in most cases the troopers felt it was their due. They had fought and suffered. Why shouldn't they take things from the Krauts? They were the legitimate 'spoils of war'. Victorious armies had always engaged in looting throughout the ages. Later when they heard about Dachau, Buchenwald and saw the evidence of Nazi terror with their own shocked eyes, they felt even more justified in their looting.

We snatched an ambulance - why, I can't remember. But when started to drive it away, we heard a cry. In the back there was a Kraut doctor trying to deliver a Kraut woman's kid! We hopped out pretty damn quick.

PVT. NORMAN NEITZKE, 101ST AB

On the fifth day of the 101st Airborne 'tour' through newly occupied southern Germany, Easy Company, 506th Parachute Infantry, stopped for the night at Buchloe, not far from the Bavarian town of Landsberg. Unknown to most of the tired troopers, Landsberg, a town of 25,000 inhabitants, was a holy place for the Nazi Party. Here back in 1924, after being sentenced to prison on account of his abortive 1923 push against the Bavarian regional government, Hitler served his time in this ugly, brown stone local jail. Not only that, it was in Landsberg Prison that the man who would become the 'Deutscher Führer' in 1933 dictated his rabble-rousing *Mein Kampf* to his 'secretary-cum-fellow inmate', Rudolf Hess, one day to become his deputy before he fled to Scotland in 1941.

But if the troopers knew little of that 'historic' site, they were unfortunate to see the results of Hitler's 1923 programme: a work camp of the notorious Dachau Concentration Camp. Most of the inmates had fled, but there were still enough around to shock the airborne troopers.

My first shock occurred when I walked across the first opening. At the edge of the woods, there was a bush, perhaps four feet high. Behind this bush was a skeleton in a crouching position. The skeleton wore the tattered striped purple garment of a Jewish concentration camp victim. I conjectured that he had either hidden here in order to escape, or in all modesty had gone behind the bush to go to the bathroom and had been too weak to return, and died.

KENNETH PARKER, 506TH PI

That was the first of many horrors for the young airborne trooper. He and his comrades of Company C discovered pits full of naked emaciated bodies which had not been burned but stacked there like cordwood ready to heat the furnace. They were tough, these American soldiers, in the last few months of combat they had all seen some pretty horrific sights, but these horrors beat all horrors they had experienced.

If the GIs were shocked, General Taylor was outraged. He was so angry that he made sure that the people of Landsberg, that sacred Nazi site, would never forget what their beloved Führer had done. The terror and horror he had wrought on the captive peoples of Europe (and Dachau and its feeder camps, contained not only continental Europeans, but also British soldiers who had escaped so frequently that they were sent there, too, to be secretly eliminated) should be etched on their mind's eye forever. There would never be an excuse for them to say later, 'We heard about these camps for the 'work shy and the perverts', but we didn't really know what was going on there behind the barbed wire. *Es war verboten*'.

Taylor ordered martial law to be imposed on Landsberg. That done, he issued an order that all citizens between the ages of fourteen and eighty should be rounded up. They would proceed under armed guard to the camp. Here they would be employed in clearing out the remaining corpses and give them a decent burial. They weren't going to forget the prisoners or the men who had released those who survived.

That evening about 1800 hours we saw the same crew of civilians coming back down the road from the concentration camp. Some of them were still puking.

KENNETH PARKER

Two days later the 101st was on its way once more. The men didn't know it, but they were heading for their last combat assignment of the war in Europe. None of them particularly wanted to fight again and possibly get killed at this stage of the war, but many of the 'Eagles' were angry enough at the Germans for what they had just seen at Landsberg to take that risk.

The impact of seeing those people behind that fence [of the camp] left me saying, only to myself, 'Now I know why I am here'.

CAPTAIN WINTERS, 101ST AB

Slowly the trucks carrying the 'Eagles' headed up the winding Bavarian roads towards those remote snow-capped peaks and what lay waiting for them there ...

IX

HITLER'S EAGLE'S NEST

After his unsuccessful attempt to seize power in Munich on 9th November 1923, Hitler was 'imprisoned' (he was treated by his right wing guards like an important political celebrity) as we have seen at Landsberg. From there, after his early release from captivity, he sought refuge in the Obersalzberg area, that strip of mountainous territory between Germany and his native Austria.[36] On the 'mountain' (Berg) as it became known in latter years, he rented a room in a small cottage called afterwards the 'Kampfhaus'. The reason for its name 'The Battle House' was simple. For it was here he finished off his infamous *Mein Kampf* (*My Battle*). Here, the pop-eyed, former police-spy and rabble-rouser found peace and benefactors, who were prepared to support him for he was without a job. And here the 'Führer' would relax in years to come when he wanted to get away from affairs of state in the hated Berlin.

In 1928 he was living in 'Haus Wachenfeld', as his National Socialist Workers' Party grew in power, paying a monthly rent of one hundred Reichsmark. Later he would purchase the house outright, from its owner, the widow of a wealthy Hamburg businessman. With the funds now flowing in from the sale of his *Mein Kampf* - every Nazi party member had to read it and after 1933 every married couple was given a copy as a wedding present[37] - Hitler had 'Haus Wachenfeld' rebuilt on a lavish scale. It was given the name of Berghof - 'mountain farm', and started the trend, especially after Hitler's takeover of power in 1933, among his ministers and cronies to have their own homes built on the 'mountain' so that they could become 'mountain people' and have closer access to the Führer than they would have had in Berlin.

In those first years in Obersalzburg, up to then a small farming community, with much of the local income coming in from the salt mines, which gave the mountain its name (Salz is the German word for 'salt'), much of the negotiating for the land to build these houses was carried out by Hitler's secretary, Rudolf Hess. But as his role grew in importance, he started to leave this task to his own obscure secretary: a man whose power grew enormously in the years to come and who one day would be ranked as second-in-command only to Hitler himself.

The new director of affairs on the 'Mountain' was a burly North German in his mid-thirties, who walked with his bullet head poked forward, thrusting out his pugnacious jaw most of the time, with his notepaper constantly ready in his sleeve turn-up. He had the hands of the peasant-farmer - and murderer which he had once been - with stumpy, thick, sausage fingers, as the Germans called them

(Wurstfinger), covered in long black hairs. All in all he looked like a boxer gone to seed who exuded aggression and menace. As Albert Speer, Hitler's architect, described him: 'even among so many ruthless men (i.e. Party bosses) he stood out through his brutality and coarseness'.

The new man's name was Martin Bormann, who had risen swiftly and silently, sticking to the shadows of the Party as he did all through his career, before his strange disappearance in 1945.

On the 'mountain' he had many nicknames - 'King of the Teleprinters' (because he was in charge of the place's secretaries and made good use of the girls both in and out of the office), 'The Sphinx' on account of the fact his broad Slavic face usually revealed nothing; the 'veggie meat-eater' (he purported to be a vegetarian, but in reality he ate the sausage he had hidden everywhere in his office by the pound), etc. etc. Hitler called him simply by his initials - 'MB'.

Hess had been pretty ineffectual in his dealings with the local farmers for their land on which the Party Prominenz wanted to build their chalets and houses next to the Führer's. Bormann was a different kettle of fish altogether. He was a typical pushy North German of the type disliked by the Bavarians. Traditionally they have called the type 'Saupreussen' (sow Prussians). Bormann had plenty of money from the Party coffers at his disposal, of course. There were the royalties from Hitler's book too and with an amazing piece of cheek, he convinced the German Postmaster General that the Führer had the copyright on his pictures used on German stamps and demanded a copyright fee for every stamp issued bearing Hitler's face! Nobody objected. How could they? They might well have ended up in the new concentration camp at nearby Dachau if they did.

It was the same with the local Obersalzburg farmers. Those who hesitated to sell to Bormann were threatened. Their sons, upon whom they might depend for labour on the steep-sided mountain pastures (in that part of the world, the mountain farmers stayed the whole of the summer up on the high pastures tending and guarding their precious cows) could be called up to the Army. They, themselves, might be accused of being anti-Nazi etc. etc. ...

Within a short space of time Bormann had bought up ten square kilometres of land, which was partially restricted and renamed the 'Führer Area',[38] soon to be guarded by a whole battalion of SS troops, anti-aircraft gunners and Hitler's own Bodyguard Squad.

Now the industrious Party Secretary went to work. He started to transform the whole area. First he widened the road from Berchtesgaden to the Berghof in order to bring up the thousands of labourers (later slave ones from the concentration camps too) needed for this large-scale construction of what had once been a modest mountain chalet surrounded by Alpine meadows.

Naturally Hitler's own home was a prime target for Bormann's efforts. The Berghof received another floor. Wide steps were constructed, those same steps upon which Hitler's victims, such as Chamberlain and the Duke and Duchess of Windsor and others, were so often photographed being received by a fawning Führer. A hall in the Gothic fashion with heavy marble pillars formed the lobby to that famous (some would say infamous) conference room with its large picture window and its view over the opposite Untersberg mountain.

Here under the snow-capped peak of the mountain, legend had it that the great Frankish King Charlemagne slept (others maintained it was the famed Stauffen Emperor Barbarossa, named after his great red beard), waiting for the moment when he would be called to restore Germany's greatness. As Hitler often told his guests, 'You see the Untersberg over there. It's no accident that I have my residence opposite it'. Naturlich!

In addition, the ground floor was refurbished and, to a certain extent, rebuilt to contain the hall, vestibule, guard room, dining room, kitchen, outside terrace in the Bavarian style and day room for his army, navy, air force and SS adjutants: all handsome men well over six feet tall.

Then there was the dining room, bedroom (the holy of holies once Hitler's mistress Eva Braun took up residence), study, and, on the second floor, rooms for semi-permanent guests. Other guests were accommodated in local pensions and hotels. These alterations, commenced back in peacetime, went on right up to 1941. After 1939 it was forbidden to build anything save structures essential to the war industry and the military. But naturally Bormann, or the 'Brown Eminence',[39] as he was being called, found a way around that particular restriction, like he did with everything that stood in the way of achieving his objective: *to be the person through whom everything and everyone had to go if he waned anything from the Führer!*

Of all the projects that Bormann carried out on the 'Mountain', the so-called 'Tea House' on the top of the Kehlstein Mountain became the best known. It was commenced immediately the Reichsleiter

(Bormann's office title) was finished with the Berghof and naturally his own house. After all that was his 'raison d'etre' - to be as close as possible to Hitler.

Some have said that Bormann undertook this grandiose scheme because he wanted to deal with the Führer 'unter vier Augen' [40] in a place where he wouldn't be disturbed by the latter's cronies and courtiers as was the case at the Berghof. Others maintain it was a present to impress Hitler. Here the Führer would be able to impress important foreign visitors and diplomats in a lone house perched on the top of a great mountain peak. Whatever the reason, Bormann now embarked on the project which would become the famed 'Eagle's Nest".

It was a major engineering feat. First a road had to be blasted out of the mountainside. This road, which would be four miles long, despite Bormann's seemingly never-ending financial resources, would never be used in winter. It would be either snowbound or too dangerous - rock fall, ice etc. Even today that same ruling applies. Still Bormann did his best. His engineers constructed it, trying to keep the number of hairpin bends in the road to a minimum, by laying the foundations through several long tunnels. Finally the road ended at a parking lot beneath the Kehlstein's peak. Here a ten-foot high tunnel ran into the mountain itself to the celebrated lift. The lift, brass lined, would take the visitor up three hundred and fifty feet to the 'Eagle's Nest", its power supplied by a bank of U-Boat engines!

All in all, the 'Eagle's Nest" presented to Hitler as a supposedly 'surprise' birthday present by a fawning Bormann on his 50th birthday on 20th April 1939, exactly six years and eleven days before he would commit suicide in this far-off bunker in Berlin, cost thirty million Reichsmark, paid by the German taxpayer. Unknown to them, they even shelled out for a *brass-lined kennel* for Hitler's favourite Alsation bitch, 'Blondi', which, too, would die in Berlin with her master among the 'sow Prussians'.

Ironically enough, although Bormann took 'tea' (more likely the fierce North German schnapps 'Schlichte' which he favoured) in the Eagle's Nest' several times on his off-day, Sunday, the Führer, for whom it was built at such great expense - and the loss of several workers' lives - visited the place exactly *five* times!

In the years that followed, Bormann, who now spent more and more time at Hitler's headquarters and Berlin, where the inveterate skirt-chaser always had new mistresses, continued his construction work on the 'Mountain'.

140

Barracks, gyms, a 2000-seat cinema, etc. etc. were all constructed, while all about one great German city after another was bombed into ruins by the RAF and the US Air Force. Even after the catastrophic defeats of El Alamein and Stalingrad, which signalled the end of the Third Reich in 1942/43, made no difference. Bormann, with the power of the whole Nazi 'apparat' at his fingertips, always managed to find the money and manpower to keep up his building programme. The ruined cities and the Armed Forces were crying out for men and materials. That didn't worry Bormann. He was too intent on pleasing the Führer and building this Potemkin village in the idyllic Bavarian Alps, far away from the strife of war.

Indirectly - and directly - Hitler knew about this mismanagement at a time when he personally was down to ordering single battalions or troops of tanks around in order to make best use of the Army's ever-diminishing resources. But as he always said to those courtiers who were honest - or daring enough - to complain about the Reichsleiter's activities on the 'mountain', 'It's all Bormann's doing. I don't want to interfere,' often adding, 'When it's finished, I'll look for a quiet valley and build another small wooden house here like the first one'.

But that was in the future. In those last days of peace when Hitler still plotted to become master of Europe, if necessary by force, life in the little idyll that Bormann had created was pleasant and lazy, very pleasant indeed. A typical day on the 'mountain' would commence at eleven o'clock. Then Hitler received his daily reports on Party affairs and local problems from Bormann. Again it was part and parcel of the Reichsleiter's strategy to keep these meetings 'among four eyes', i.e., between himself and Hitler. Thereafter came an extended 'Mittagessen', the main midday dinner in the German working class fashion. Bormann would have the honour of escorting Hitler's mistress, Eva Braun, the former assistant of the Führer's personal photographer, 'Professor' Heinrich Hoffmann,[41] to the table. This, according to Speer, a frequent guest at these long drawn out lunches, 'was proof of Bormann's dominant position in the court'.

The food was always simple, though always throat-burningly hot. Hitler, however, was very pedantic about the service and grew exceedingly angry with the uniformed servants (mostly from the SS and of officer rank; his butler was, for example, a colonel in the SS), if even a fork was in the wrong place.

Beer and wine were served in spite of Hitler's suppose dislike of alcohol. Meat was also on offer for those who wished to partake of it.

Naturally Bormann took neither in deference to his master, though Hitler probably had a shrewd idea that his secretary, who was growing increasingly thick around the waist, enjoyed both alcohol and meat.

The son of Heinrich Hoffmann, also a photographer-to-be, remembers Bormann hiding a sausage behind a cupboard in his office. After a meal he would rush to the office, lock the door and hastily cutting off a slice of salami, would gobble it down greedily.

Richard Schulze, a friend of Bormann's brother-in-law, an SS Officer, who was generally regarded as something of a comedian in the Berghof circle, once told Hitler, to his face: 'You have a lot of hypocrites around you, mein Führer'.

Surprised, Hitler asked him what he meant.

Schulze replied: 'People who pretend to be vegetarians like yourself, but stuff themselves with sausage. I call them 'fried sausage vegetarians (Bratwurstvegetarier)'.

'Who do you mean,' Hitler queried.

Schulze refused to name names. If I told you, mein Führer, he replied, 'I'd be kicked out of the Party'.

Hitler smiled now. 'I think I know *who* you mean,' was his sole comment before dropping the subject.

After their extended midday dinner, the intimate group of hangers-on usually went for a stroll to the teahouse, ascending up a narrow path.

This was much to Bormann's annoyance. He didn't like this two at a time 'procession', as Speer called it. He wanted to prevent anyone getting on too intimate terms with the Führer for he was really what the Germans call a 'Radfahrer' (a cyclist): one who kicks those below him and pays homage to those above in the manner that cycle pedals move. He would have wished the whole group to have made use of his road where such intimacies would have been avoided.

In summer the group met outside in the meadows, flirting and dozing as they listened to the Führer's interminable monologues. In the wintertime they gathered around the roaring log fire in the great fireplace, drinking tea, or coffee, or even sipping the local liqueurs (Hitler preferred peppermint tea).

Here again the Führer was fond of 'drifting into endless monologues', as Speer put it, on subjects as familiar to himself and his guests that they often fell asleep while listening. Occasionally Hitler even drifted into sleep personally. Then his young mistress, the sporty, empty-headed Eva Braun would continue the conversation in a hushed voice and everyone pretended - sycophants that they were - that Hitler was wide awake and still listening.

There in the teahouse at the top of the world, or so it seemed, the 'court' bored with themselves and Hitler, would spend a couple of hours until the Führer's black Mercedes, complete with heavily armed thuggish bodyguard, would arrive and spirit him away to the Berghof. Then, probably sighing with relief, the party could act normally for a while. They could flirt, indulge in court gossip, drink German champagne (no French muck at Hitler's court; it always had to be *Sekt*, the German sparkling wine), and generally let their hair down. The Reichsleiter was no exception. Although his usually pregnant wife, Gerda, lived less than a mile away, he would enjoy the favours of one of the females who worked for him. As Speer noticed, 'Bormann disappeared into the room [below] of one of the younger stenographers which elicited spiteful remarks from Eva Braun'.

But Eva kept those remarks to those who like herself hated Martin Bormann. Even the Führer's mistress knew that Reichsleiter Bormann was not a man to cross; he was such a powerful person in the Party. However, she did like Bormann's long-suffering wife Gerda. She considered her a good friend. But again she was angry at Bormann for the way he treated her. Not only did he flaunt his current girlfriend in front of her, but he also kept her permanently pregnant, even when in the end she was suffering from the cancer of the womb which killed her.

Bormann refused to allow his wife to wear lipstick or smoke, true to the Nazi precept that a 'German woman neither smokes or makes herself up'. Indeed in general he treated Gerda like German men had handled their wives in the bad old days of the three 'K's – 'Kinder, Kueche und Kirche' (children, kitchen and church).

The evening meal at the Berghof was announced by telephone. The phone calls summoned the courtiers to eat. But first they assembled in the long hall-lounge at eight in the evening before heading for the dining room. Again it was the same boring routine, save that the burningly hot dishes of dinner which Hitler preferred were replaced by cold cuts and salads, plus lots of bread in the traditional German fashion. The conversation once more was banal and boring. 'Your napkin is stained with lipstick,' Hitler would chide Eva, who sat next to him, mildly. 'What are you painting yourself with?'

Then he, as he always did, would remark when Eva would protest the lipstick was very expensive and came all the way from Paris, that 'Ah, if you ladies only knew what French lipstick is made from - *the grease of kitchen slops!*' Hereupon he would laugh, hiding his mis-shapen teeth and bridge with his napkin.

The reaction would be giggles of disbelief from the ladies present, mostly secretaries, whose hands he would insist on kissing when they left, in the style of an old Austrian aristocrat.

Towards midnight when his forced guests were beginning to yawn wearily, after the usual film, they would all sit and listen to the phono-graph in front of the fire in the great hall. Hitler selected the records personally. Although he was supposedly a great fan of Wagner, for these evening 'concerts' he selected the same old favourites: Strauss, Lehar and the like, those frothy compositions of Austrian-Hungarian composers dating back to the 'fin de siecle'.

Then finally the ordeal was over. Just as so many newly elected European governments and their hangers-on had enjoyed the fruits of the take-over, looting their newly-acquired national riches with greedy paws, Hitler and his like had spent another day at the trough. They had produced nothing, save so much hot air. But bored as they may well have been, those jumped-up little people from the provinces with little talent and less experience, had arrived. The 'New Germany', as they insisted on calling it ('new' in politics had, it appears, survived even unto our own time) was their oyster and they were determined to enjoy it as long as they could.

As Speer, bright but just as much a toady as the rest, put it: 'In the early hours of the morning we went home dead tired, exhausted from doing nothing. After a few days of this, I was seized by what I called at the time 'the mountain sickness'. That is, I felt exhausted and vacant from the constant waste of time...'

With the coming of the war in 1939, one year after Chamberlain, the British Prime Minister had himself been greeted by the Führer at the Berghof during the former's futile attempt to save the peace at Munich, austerity - of a kind - descended upon Obersalzberg. Still whenever he could, Hitler accompanied by the toadying Bormann, would return there. Again the usual routine would commence, the war apparently forgotten. After all these early years were those of Germany's victories. She seemed unstoppable. The only sign of war were the young officers who had been awarded medals for bravery and had been invited to spend the weekend at Obersalzberg as the Führer's guests.

Naturally security was tightened. The usual crowds of civilians who had come by train and bus to file respectfully by the Berghof, deliberately kept modest - *on the outside* - to impress them with the Führer's modest style of living, ceased after 1st September 1939. Now fighter planes patrolled the Alpine skies above the resort and an anti-aircraft battalion was dug in to defend the place against an enemy air attack.

Then Bormann - secretary at first - started his own private tunnel beneath the rock against any such aerial assault. Goering, who had boasted he would be called 'Meier' (a supposedly Jewish name), if any enemy plane crossed the frontiers of the Reich, followed in 1941. He requested that his tunnel should be linked to that built by Bormann. The Reichsleiter refused 'Fat Hermann's' request and so the two tunnels remained separated by thirty feet of rock. In the end all of the Prominenz got into the act, demanding underground protection, with air conditioning, with Eva Braun asking for her own private bedroom away 'from the mob'. As yet, however, not a single allied bomb had been dropped on the place. But the tide of the war was turning and the British RAF was already flying long-distance raids above the Alps to bomb Italian targets followed by a landing in North Africa. Soon they would be able to bomb from Southern Italy itself.

By the winter of 1945, with Nazi Germany fighting desperately for survival, Obersalzberg was virtually abandoned by the 'Prominenz'. Hitler was fighting the Battle of the Bulge from his 'front line' headquarters at Ziegenberg and Bormann, now the most powerful man in the dying Third Reich after the Führer, drank and whored and vainly attempted to keep the structure of the '1000 Year Reich' alive from Berlin.

But although the big shots were absent from the 'Mountain', it had become of vital importance to the Allies. For sources reporting to the US spymaster, Allen Dulles, the future head of the CIA, in Switzerland were convinced that the Nazis would make a last stand in the area, in what was to become known as the 'National Redoubt'.

Here in the Alps between Austria, Germany and German-held Italy, the diehard Nazis would make their last defiant battle against the Anglo-Americans. According to Dulles' agents, the elite of the Wehrmacht and Waffen SS were already moving into the area. Slave labour was constructing fortification everywhere in the mountains (Bormann's tunnels?). Soon the new Nazi underground movement, der Werwolf, would sally forth and start assassinating the traitors and lickspittles who were now working for the enemy.

In the end the whole National Redoubt of 'Alpine Fortress', as it was sometimes also called, turned out to be a myth. There were no elite SS troops prepared to make a last ditch stand in the Obersalzberg area. As for the mysterious 'Werwolf', it was, as one German called the organisation contemptuously, 'nothing but a rabble of boy scouts' ...

On Wednesday 25th April 1945, 'Butcher' Harris, as the chief of the RAF's Bomber Command was known - *behind his back* - alerted his crews to show the world that he was going to be in at the death of that hated country which his bombers had effectively ruined. Once back in 1942, Harris, speeding in his big American car to his underground headquarters at High Wykeham, had been stopped by a young bobby for driving too fast in a thirty mile an hour zone.

The policeman, not recognising the high-ranking RAF officer with his rows of medals and bristling moustache set against a testy angry mouth, lectured the Air Vice Marshal: 'You'll be killing somebody one day if you keep driving at this speed'. Harris didn't bat an eyelid. Sternly he replied, 'Young man, *I* kill *thousands* of people every night'. And so he probably did. Now on this Wednesday, he was going to kill some more, including, if he was lucky, no less a person than Adolf Hitler himself. For so far Allied Intelligence had no idea of the Führer's whereabouts. Their best guess was that he fled to the 'National Redoubt' to fight to the end. Where would his quarters be, if he had done so? Naturally the Berghof on Bormann's mountain.

For the RAF's 617th Squadron, four-engined Lancasters, some of them carrying the same massive bombs that had smashed the German Moehne Dam the previous year, began their slow ascent above and then across the Alps. Their objective - Berchtesgaden and Obersalzberg.

On the 'mountain' the first dreaded whine of the air raid sirens, sounding what the Germans called the 'Voralarm' (preliminary warning), commenced at nine thirty that fine morning. Hastily the inhabitants, flunkeys, slave workers and conscripted German ones, doubled for the shelters which Bormann had constructed two years before. Not a moment too soon.

At ten o'clock the first planes were directly overhead. By now the target had become obscured by ground mist and the fact that some snow had fallen during the night. Still the navigators and bomb-aimers pressed on. The first 1,000 lb bombs fell on the housing estates at Buchenhoehe and Klaushoehe. The earth trembled under their impact like a live thing. Still the hundreds of frightened civilians sheltering in the air-raid bunkers were relatively safe (save for a direct hit) behind their steel doors, blast-proof walls and even gas locks. For Bormann's engineers had thought of everything, even the employment of poison gas by the Anglo-American 'air pirates' (as German propaganda called them).

Thirty minutes later the second wave of Lancasters came lumbering in. The planes sprang high in the air as they released their heavy loads. For a solid half hour, the RAF's 617 Squadron bombed the 'mountain'. Then finally they disappeared to the west, leaving behind them the cherry-red of fires everywhere and a black mushroom of smoke slowly descending up above the Alpine peaks.

It wasn't a particularly successful raid, due to weather conditions. Still the RAF had dropped over 1,200 tons of high explosive within the space of an hour, including the massive 12,000 pounders. The RAF's publicists at the London Air Ministry announced the following Thursday that the 'Führer's Retreat' had become 'a heap of ruins', while 'not one stone of the SS barracks was left upon another'.

The report was not exactly true, but one side of the Berghof had been completely destroyed and both Goering's and Bormann's houses were badly damaged, as were the barracks of the <u>Waffen SS</u> guard battalion and the Platterhof, soon to be used by the victorious Americans as a holiday hotel. The loss of life, too, was very slight. Out of the 3,500 people sheltering in Bormann's tunnels, a mere six were killed.

Yet Bormann's 'mountain' was about finished. The commander of the SS on Obersalzberg had already told the civilian and military authorities down below in Berchtesgaden that he and his men didn't intend to defend the 'mountain'. They were going to withdraw south to meet up with the Sixth SS Army, or what was left of it, retreating through Austria in front of the pursuing Red Army.

Immediately widespread looting broke out on the 'mountain'. Germans and non-Germans started to plunder the huge supplies of food, cigarettes, clothes and goods left behind by the 'mountain people', now the SS were moving out. It was every man for himself. Everyone knew the shortages that would occur once the Allies were finally victorious. Why should they feed and clothe the beaten Germans who had caused so much death, misery and suffering throughout Europe in these last five and a half years? As they quipped cynically to one another in those final days of the great world conflict, 'geniesse den Krieg, der Frieden wird schrecklich sein' (enjoy the war, the peace is going to be terrible). Here and there the withdrawing SS started to stop them, firing bursts over the mob's heads. But in the end, they, too, gave up. On Friday 4th May, as the Americans began coming up the mountain roads, they gave up. In one last burst of what the Germans call in that untranslatable phrase of theirs: 'schadenfreude',[42] the SS poured the last of their petrol over the Berghof and then proceeded to set Hitler's home on fire ...

X

ATTACK ON THE EAGLE'S NEST

Now the troopers under that veteran Col. Sink entered the supposed last-ditch fortress, the 'Alpine Redoubt'. We know that it did not exist, but Col. Sink and his paratroopers didn't know that. Perhaps the more imaginative of them felt they would be confronted by al kinds of 'V-weapons', as the Nazis called their new secret revenge weapons such as the V-1, V-2 and V-3.[43] What might be V-4? Some terrible poison gas against which no gas mask was proof?

The battered German prisoners in their shapeless, ankle-length greatcoats now filing past the 'Eagles' to the rear didn't seem very formidable. But the fanatical SS might be a different kettle of fish altogether.

> We looked at each other with great curiosity. I am sure both armies shared one thought - 'Oh just let me alone. All I want is to get this over with and go home'.
> CAPTAIN WINTERS VIEWING GERMAN POWS

That Thursday with the threat of snow in the air above the mountains, Sink's paratroopers prepared for the last advance. During the night more urgent orders came in, urging Sink to collect extra ammunition and rations. Obviously General Taylor expected trouble. At the same time they were commanded to move at 0600 hrs. They'd take the autobahn to Salzburg and then switch from the Austrian border town back into Germany and Berchtesgaden.

The excited and apprehensive 101st troopers didn't know the reason for the change of timing and the order to use the autobahn. But they did understand the need for extra ammo. There was going to be a fight. There was, but not the kind they anticipated. Their fight was not really to take place between them and the Germans, but against their allies: the troops of General 'Iron Mike' O'Daniel's 3rd US Infantry Division and General LeClerc's 2nd French Armored Division.

The 101st considered itself an elite division, but in the Third 'the Rock of the Marne'[44] and the French Second, it was matched against two formations which had unrivalled combat experience. LeClerc's Free French had commenced their battle back in Africa in 1941 and, with American help, they had captured both Paris and Strasbourg. O'Daniel, who had lost his nineteen year old son as a paratrooper in Holland, commanded a division, which had fought in North Africa, Italy, France and Germany. The Third had won more Congressional Medals than any other US outfit in Europe, including that won by future movie star Audie Murphy. O'Daniel considered if any outfit was going to have the honour of capturing Hitler's 'Eagle's Nest", it should be his.

LeClerc, under sentence of death still from his own 'official' govern-ment,[45] felt pretty much the same.

Naturally while O'Daniel raced ahead for the prestige of the Third, which had earned its nickname 'The Rock of the Marne', helping to defend France back in the trenches in World War One, LeClerc was taking his orders, in part, from de Gaulle. De Gaulle, running a shaky government in Paris, wanted a symbolic victory to end the war for France, which had been defeated in 1940, occupied by the Germans for four years, until it was finally liberated by the Anglo-Americans in 1944. The Second Armored raced ahead, knowing that there was more at stake than drinking 'Old Adolf's champagne wine'.

We pushed on very fast in competition with the Americans. We were operating in groups again and ours had a pretty straight run through with only odd spots of opposition... Everybody seemed to be waving white flags and nobody knew anything about Hitler.
EMIL G. FRAY, 2ND FRENCH ARMORED DIVISION

Naturally the Top Brass didn't like the French General's high-handed manner. After all, he was under American command and was being supplied by the US Army. In the eyes of higher headquarters, LeClerc had to obey orders like every other subordinate commander (not that American 'Iron Mike' was obeying them very much in this crazy, excited and sometimes dangerous last week of the shooting war!).

I soon lost him [LeClerc]... Suddenly there was a telephone call from a divisional commander [O'Daniel], complaining that the French had appeared and were getting in the way. I said, "Just you block the roads and that will stop them".
CORPS COMMANDER GEN. WADE HAISLIP AFTER THE WAR

General O'Daniel did as his corps commander suggested. He or-dered his 'Marnemen' to guard all the bridges over the River Saalach. The river would form an effective barrier to anyone attempting to slip through and reach the Eagle's Nest first. Now it was LeClerc's turn to make a complaint to the higher headquarters. He broke radio silence and appealed to Haislip. The big bluff, rotund Corps Commander, who had attended military schools in pre-war France and was a francophile, told the aristocratic Frenchman, who had relinquished his title and real name in 1940 for a 'nom-de-guerre' that he too had to obey or-ders.

You aren't supposed to be there at all. You've had Paris and you've had Strasbourg. You can't expect Berchtesgaden as well.
GEN. HAISLIP TO GEN. LECLERC 5TH MAY 1945

Meanwhile, as O'Daniel and LeClerc fought their private battle, Colonel Sink's paratroopers kept a low profile. Sink wanted Berchtesgaden as much as the other two did. But he wasn't going to suffer unnecessary casualties at this late stage of the war; his regiment were not to take unnecessary chances. Reluctantly the younger troopers out for loot and 'frauleins' impatient to lose their virginity, obeyed. The troops passed through Rosenheim and on to Chiemsee. The scenery was spectacular. Not even the sleet that came down in sheets now and again could hide the beauty of the Alps. At Siegsdorf, the leading elements of the 'Screaming Eagles' turned right onto the highway that led directly to Berchtesgaden.

Now they bumped into the French. For a whole day LeClerc's men out for 'La Gloire' were stalled. The retreating Germans had blown up a bridge across a deep ravine. The 2nd Armored Division lacked bridging equipment. Right throughout the campaign they had begged, borrowed and stolen from their American comrades-in-arms. Now the Americans weren't so forthcoming. Besides, on the other side of the ravine, a party of SS had dug in and were peppering the stalled troops with small arms fire. Sink wouldn't attack, as he might have done normally. He said, 'I don't want anyone hurt'. Instead he decided to attempt to outflank the roadblock. He sent his Second Battalion back along the autobahn in an attempt to find another way into Berchtesgaden. His last words to the battalion commander were: 'Reserve the Berchtesgaden Hof for the Regimental HQ'. It was that kind of battle!

Meanwhile LeClerc was bringing up the bulk of his division to complete the final kilometres to Berchtesgaden. He paused to catch a couple of dozen renegade Frenchmen being shot by his troops. The hangdog renegades had fought with the SS Division Charlemagne for the Germans. LeClerc, who had been sentenced to death for treachery by the same French government which had allowed these young Frenchmen to join an SS division and fight for the 'Boche', had no hesitation about having them shot out of hand. (Today they are buried at the cemetery of Bad Reichenhall, a few kilometres from Berchtesgaden). Then it was on again, trying to beat the Americans for the final victory.

I was racing ahead with the General... when on two separate occasions American military police on traffic patrol tried to stop me. LeClerc told me to drive right through them... and make them jump. I did -*and they did!*

Col. Chatel, 2nd French Armored Division

But it wasn't only LeClerc's Frenchmen who were being stalled by their comrades-in-arms of the 3rd Division. Colonel Strayer's 2nd Battalion of the 506th Parachute Infantry Regiment was having trouble too. The Battalion had doubled back, as ordered to by Colonel Sink. They had successfully crossed the Saalbahn, a dirt road through the 3rd Division area. But they needed to bring up bridging equipment for their motorized transport to continue. But that wasn't to be. At the head of the dirt road they found another roadblock. This one was commanded by no less a person than 'Iron Mike' of the Third. And the General was not allowing anyone to beat his Marnemen to Berchtesgaden. The 'Screaming Eagles' were stalled too.

LeClerc had a short fuse. He knew more than just the capture of a small Bavarian town was at stake. The capture of Berchtesgaden was more than this. It might well wipe out the terrible stigma of France's defeat in June 1940. He tried to contact O'Daniel, just as Colonel Sink was doing. No deal! The commander of the 'Rock of the Marne' Division wasn't answering the phone.

Everybody and his brother are trying to get into that town today.

Signal from XXI Corps, 6th May 1945

While LeClerc and presumably Colonel Sink fumed, O'Daniel waited on tenterhooks. He had disobeyed orders. The French and the paratroopers had been given the task of capturing Berchtesgaden, not his Third. Still he had two bridges on his hands and his Seventh Infantry in place. If he captured Hitler's holiday home, all would be well. If he attempted and failed, all hell would be let loose. But now he took a chance.

Colonel Heintges was ordered into the attack across the Saalach bridges. They were to be heavily guarded so that no one else could use them. So with his rear covered, the Colonel and his Seventh advanced upon the holy of holies. They knew the place was defended by the SS but Heintges needn't have worried. The SS were drunk and busy looting and burning, trying to wreck the Nazi mountain complex about Berchtesgaden before the Americans arrived. Besides, the local council were determined to surrender to the enemy without a fight.

Everything went according to plan. The Seventh took Berchtesgaden and now everything was over, barring the shouting - in this case, a ceremonial display of the US conquest: the traditional flag-raising ...

There are two stories extant about what happened next. What is clear is that the French of LeClerc's Division did manage to block the roads up to the still smoking, partially ruined Nazi complex on the mountain. Thus it was the French decided they would hoist the <u>tricolour</u> above the high ground behind Goering's shattered lodge. The Americans protested and it was decided that both O'Daniel's Third and the French Second would conduct a joint ceremony in front of the newsreel camera. According to one account, everything went to plan as the cameras whirred. The one the author likes better is this: the raising of the flags, the salutes, the speeches had duly taken place with the cameramen going full out, when suddenly - surprisingly - the heavy French flag fell over. Shock, outrage, bewilderment. What happened? Had the weight of the flag been too much? Had some nasty-minded American GI sabotaged the flag of France? We shall never know. But there it was - *'Old Glory' fluttering in triumph over the lair of the Nazi Beast in solitary splendour!*

Section II

A GUIDE FOR TODAY

OLD JOLLY

The first memorial to the US troops who had trained at Slapton Sands, the many thousands who had struggled up that beach, sick, wet, weary, not realising just how much worse things would be at Utah, the real thing, was erected by the US Army just after the war. However both the British and American authorities kept the wraps on the secret of 'Operation Tiger'. Indeed the damaged villages and farms of the area were swiftly rebuilt and the locals allowed to return speedily as if to remove all traces of the tragedy.

But the rumours set off by the publication of Harry Butcher's *Three Years with Eisenhower*[46] continued to circulate. A captain in the US Medical Corps recalled how his Colonel had come into the 228th Station Hospital at Sherborne in Dorset and told him and his assembled colleagues, 'There will be no discussion. Following standard procedure, anyone who talks about casualties... will be subject to court martial. No one will be able to leave our perimeter until further orders'. The BBC started to investigate the almost forgotten tragedy. But it was a local man, Ken Small, who made the breakthrough with the discovery and recovery of a lost Sherman tank off Slapton Sands.

It took Small sixteen years to raise the tank and have it placed as a second memorial to the US servicemen who had laboured, together with the local villagers, to make a success of D-Day - at great cost to both parties. President Reagan was so impressed that he wrote Small a personal letter congratulating him on his achievement over forty years after the event.

These two memorials at Slapton are perhaps the most tangible and obvious monuments to the 101st and other divisions of Collins' VII Corps which attacked Utah. There are others, almost forgotten hardstands, landing strips, airfields etc., throughout southern England from which the airborne and seaborne troops set out. One of the 101st Airborne departure fields is now a service station on the M4 motorway. At another one (4th Division this time) a bitter battle is currently being fought between British Normandy Veterans and the local council to prevent it being turned into a housing development. A third is the Boston Boatyard at Oreston, Plymouth, where the two landing crafts, used by Spielberg in his epic *Saving Private Ryan* were built in the late '90s. History repeating itself in a way.

But to find them depends a lot on local knowledge and even when they are found, they tend to be disappointing due to the fact that after half a century or more they had been integrated into existing structures. However, for the student of World War Two, a 'must' is definitely a visit to Southwick House just behind the great former naval port of Portsmouth.

It was here in the great 18th century mansion and the surrounding terrain that those last minute vital decisions about D-Day were made. General Eisenhower, the Supreme Commander, parked his great 'trailer home' close to the place's Pinsley Lodge (up to recently its hard-pad of concrete was still visible). In the grounds, 'Monty' and his HQ staff of two hundred and twenty officers and men were billeted in two caravans and tents; while most of the huge Supreme Commander's staff worked in the house itself.

Naturally the whole area was a 'no-go' area in that spring of '44, though the locals knew of the 'big shots' coming and going all the time. One unfortunate noncom even managed to post his sister in Chicago a batch of 'OVERLORD' (the code-name for D-Day) documents, which slipped out in the Chicago postal sorting office. He's probably still in jail!

Here after writing that never-to-be published dispatch that he and he alone was responsible for any failure of the D-Day landings, Eisenhower left. Where did he go? Why, to see off a bunch of 'Screaming Eagles' flying from Greenham Common Airfield in middle England (still there). He knew that they were the bravest of the brave and that if anyone needed encouragement (for, if the attack failed, they would be totally isolated in France and wiped out), it was these young men with the black and white eagles of the US 101st Airborne Division on their shoulder, who feature in that evocative photograph of 'Ike' and his troops on the eve of D-Day.

How to get there

From London, the easiest way is from Waterloo Station to Kingsbridge (Devon). Here there are local buses, rather infrequent, running the dozen miles or so from Kingsbridge to Slapton Village. There in front of you is the Mere and the 'invasion beach' with its two monuments to the war, plus the recovered Sherman tank.

To your rear, looking from the beach, you can see across the marshy area around the Mere, thought by the planners to be similar to that of the area in France in which the 'Screaming Eagles' would drop and fight. Beyond are the heights where, unwittingly, the men of the 101st were witness to the tragic outcome of 'Operation Exercise Tiger'.

From Slapton retrace your steps by the same method by rail (or road, naturally) to Portsmouth. The one-time great British naval base is still worth a one-day visit, especially if the battlefield tourist is taking the midnight ferry to France to visit the 101st's other battlefields in Europe. For the general visitor there is Nelson's flagship, the 'Victory', and for the American one, Portsmouth's celebrated 'Pilgrim Trail', dedicated to the first of the 'Founding Fathers'. Indeed there can be no better place to set sail for the trail that leads from the Beaches to Berchtesgaden. Just as the 'Pilgrims' went forth from here into the unknown, so did the 'American Eagles' all those years ago ...

NORMANDY

There are monuments, memorials, museums to the 'Screaming Eagles' and their comrades of the 82nd Airborne Division, the 'All Americans' virtually everywhere in that part of France which contained the Utah and Omaha beaches landing sites. But due to the confusion of the drop and the fearful over-reaction of some of the pilots who dropped them, they are widely scattered. Often times they are a mere plaque in a wall or a name on some village street, which is meaningless to most visitors. But for the battlefield tourist, eager to trace the main stages of the flight of the 'American Eagles' through war-torn Europe, it is suggested that they stick to the most significant and most accessible of these sites.

Perhaps it might be best to start on this trail once taken by 'Spielberg's Eagles' where the master himself opened his celebrated first 101st AB movie, *Saving Private Ryan* at the <u>Normandy Cemetery</u>.

It is situated on a cliff overlooking Omaha Beach and the Channel. It is just east of <u>St Laurent-sur-Mer</u>. The cemetery, covering one hundred and seventy-two acres, contains the graves of 9,386 American soldiers. Here there is a grave of a real Private Ryan, killed with the 101st AB on 6th June 1944, plus that of the two Preston T. Niland, killed on D-I with the Fourth Division's 22nd Inf. Rgt. and Robert, who was killed on D-Day with the 101st sister outfit, the 82nd 'All American' Airborne Division.

Just beyond the great and sad cemetery to young American soldiers who still rest in a foreign land that they came to liberate nearly sixty years ago now, there is the <u>Utah Beach Monument</u> three kilometres north-east of <u>St Marie-du-Mont</u>, overlooking the US VII Corps' celebrated beach which was cleared by midday on 6th June. Ironically the casualties incurred there in the real battle were one sixth of those taken in the mock one at Slapton Sands during 'Operation Tiger'.

While in the area of Utah and Omaha beaches, it might interest the visitor to have a look at a little known historical curiosity of that June battle. It is that monument dedicated to one of Britain's least known and unsung irregular forces, who commenced the battle of the beaches nearly two years *before* D-Day.

It is that to the 'Small Scale Raiding Force' ((SSRF), working for a top secret intelligence organisation created by Churchill himself in the black days of 1940 with the instruction 'Set Europe Ablaze'. This

Special Operations Executive (SOE) ordered a small bunch of the SSRF commandos under the command of a Major Gus March-Phillips to reconnoitre the beach of Omaha on the night of 12th September 1942. The results of their findings about the beach were to be used by the American planners for the D-Day assault.

Unfortunately the eight-man team found the beach to be heavily mined and patrolled before they ran into a party of the enemy. A running fire-fight ensued and Major March-Phillips ordered his men to withdraw to their boats, while he searched the bodies of the dead Germans for information. Just about then the commando unit hit another German patrol. The Major was killed in the fire-fight and three of his men were captured. Two escaped. One swam along the beach and contacted the French Resistance which smuggled him through Occupied France and with freedom in sight, he was captured. Franco's Spanish police handed him over to the Germans. Later he was shot by a firing squad. What was left of this special unit was then incorporated into the British SAS.

Today the small faded memorial to those brave and ill-fated forerunners of the D-Day heroes is a plaque on the front of Omaha Beach. It is worth a visit to remember those men and all the other 'backroom boys' who prepared for the great invasion for months, even years...

Slightly inland and in between the two American beaches, Utah and Omaha, there is 'The Airborne Museum' at St Mere-Eglise, fittingly dedicated to the two celebrated US airborne divisions, the 101st and 82nd, which played such an important role in the success of the landings.

Here we can see some of the famed incidents of that terrible, if glorious 6th June, 1944. There is 'Rupert Dummy', used as a decoy of the day. There is too a very vivid reconstruction nearby of that poor trooper who had his parachute snagged on the steeple of the village church and hung there all night, feigning dead, while a vicious fire fight went on just below him. And for those World War Two 'buffs' interested in the hardware of the D-Day battle in the Museum's 'Batiment 2' (Building Two) there is a C-47 which supposedly took part in the operation. Not far away on the plinth in front of Building Two there is also a wartime Sherman Tank to remind visitors that the 'poor bloody infantry' of the 4th Infantry Division, 'The Ivy League', played their part in the great enterprise too.

In that general area of some twenty square miles, there are monuments enough to the 'Screaming Eagles' - General Taylor's first CP;

the 'Cabbage Patch', where so much bloody fighting took place etc. etc. The French, after all, although reluctant to display the real extent of their debt to the Anglo-Americans who liberated their country, have known how to market 'D-Day'. But for this author the most poignant of these memorials (apart from the one to those long forgotten commandos of 1942), is that to the ill-fated General Pratt. What had he known that 4th June 1944 when he had rounded on the officer who had carelessly thrown his cap on Pratt's bed? Had he guessed what was going to happen to him? We don't know. But what we do know is this: although he never fired a shot in anger in his whole long military career, General Pratt was fated to be the first general officer to die in the campaign in Europe. Ironically enough, it is some sort of claim to fame, isn't it?

BASTOGNE I

The best way to follow the course of the first half of the Battle for Bastogne is to travel eastwards from the town itself until one reaches the Highway N-7 between Luxembourg-St. Vith. Parallel to it in the valley below runs the River Our. Here between Stolzemburg and Dasburg, one can see the weir, where in September 1944, the first US troops of the 5th Armored Division, first entered Germany in WWII. At this same spot along the length of the River till Dasburg, von Luettwitz's Panzerkorps' assault the western heights with N-7 Highway topping them. This was the GIs' 'Skyline Drive'.

Each village square along this road heading north to St. Vith has its quota of heavy guns etc., recalling the time when the 110 US Infantry were decimated here. At Hosingen (the water tower is still there on the height to the right of the N-) turn off and join the country road leading to Longvilly and Magaret. Here the battlefield tourist is running parallel to the road that Bayerlein's Panzerlehr took after being allegedly misdirected b a Luxembourg farmer. While Fritz Bayerlein sorted himself out that confused night, a team from the 10th Armored established a roadblock at Longvilly. Here one might say the Battle of Bastogne commenced. Today there is little to be seen of the action save the shell-pocked walls of the older houses.

Instead of entering Bastogne here - every approach road to 'Nuts City' is guarded by the turret of a wartime Sherman tank, armed with a 75 mm canon, turn off to Clervaux on the N-18 country road. At the Hotel Claravallis (with US flag outside) you can see the HQ of the ill-fated 110 Inf. Rgt., while at the ruined castle, which was defended by men of that regiment during the battle before the castle went up in flames, you find the museum devoted to the 28th Infantry Division 'the Bloody Bucket.[47]

From there onto 'Nuts City' itself with its numerous monuments and displays, in particular the great Battle of the Bulge museum, a state-of-the-arts site which just has to be visited.

But for this particular writer, the most interesting Bastogne monument is that of Place McAuliffe, where in front of the wartime Sherman tanks is the Bourne, the last of the 1,300 odd similar road signs, which lead across France, Luxembourg and Belgium. They were erected in 1946/47 by the local population (some of whom could hardly afford their contribution to their own particular bourne.). They were intended to thank the Americans for all time for the way they had liberated them. But the one at Bastogne has a special place in the hearts of those who knew the high cost that the 101st Airborne Division paid for that liberation. From the first one at St-Mere-Eglise to this last one at Bastogne, those stones symbolize the flight of those 'Screaming Eagles' who would never come back...

Stars representing the forty-eight stars of the USA, 1944.

Four rectangles representing the four sections of the Route of Liberation.

Name of route and date.

The flame of liberty modelled on that of the Statue of Liberty.

Kilometre mark.

Emblem of 3rd Army, commanding officer, Gen. Patton.

Waves representing the Atlantic Ocean.

Route of Liberation inaugurated in 1946 (modelled on the 'Sacred Way' to Verdun in WWI) covers the path of the US Army from Ste Mere Eglise and Utah to Bastogne with 1300 odd stones.

THE ROUTE OF THE AMERICAN EAGLES FROM BEACH TO BASTOGNE, 1944

The Dutch, being the people they are, hard-working, businesslike and thrifty, soon stated repairing the ruins of the Arnhem campaign. At Lommel, where Horrocks' British XXX Corps started its sixty-mile dash to link up with the 101st and 82nd Airborne Divisions and drive on to Arnhem, there is little to be seen to remind the visitor that this is an historic spot. For here, in a way, on 17th September 1944 the fate of Western Europe was decided for almost half a century. If the Horrocks' drive had succeeded and the war won by the end of 1944, the whole political map of Central Europe might have been totally different. But that wasn't the case.

Since that time, nature and man have had their way. All that remains of that time at Lommel are such sad memorials as the Polish and German cemeteries which lie there. However it is still worth paying a small side visit to 'Joe's Bridge', where a combined force of Irish Guards infantry - and armour - under the command of Lt. Col. 'Joe' Vakeleur set off with such high hopes that they would link up with the 'Yanks' of the 101st AB by later afternoon.

'Joe's Bridge' over the Canal has been naturally rebuilt. In 1940 the retreating Belgian Army destroyed it. Then it was replaced by a wooden structure, built under German command. That structure was nearly blown again in September '44, but a brave British engineer major saved it by rushing the bridge just in time. A week or so later the man in question, Major Peel, was killed in a German counter-attack. The place now known as 'Joe's Bridge' has a violent wartime history.

Through its central span, from the right of the slip road approach from which most visitors take their pictures, you can see the factory where Horrocks and his staff watched the start of the great operation from its roof. What thoughts must have gone through his head at that moment? 'He wasn't a well man. He had been wounded several times and had been a prisoner-of-war twice. But undoubtedly being Horrocks (or 'Jorrocks', as he was known to his men), he would have tossed any grave thoughts to one side in his give-away style with some joke or quip.

On to <u>Valkenswaard</u>. It is seventeen kilometres from 'Joe's Bridge' and as far as Horrocks' Guards were able to penetrate on 17th September. All day the 'Micks' had been fighting off counter-attacks on the 'Corridor' ('Hell's Highway' to the 'Screaming Eagles') by two battalions of the 9th SS Panzer Division. Unfortunately for the overall success of the 'Market Garden' operation, the Guards refuelled and stayed the night at Valkenswaard before setting off at six the next morning.

Ahead of them went the armoured cars of the Household Cavalry. They found the site roads impossible. So they circled around Eindhoven and set the 101st AB's 606th Parachute Infantry Regiment north of the city at Woenscel. Here they contacted General Taylor. The latter told them that the bridge at Son had been damaged; he needed engineers immediately. "Phone us", he told the surprised British cavalrymen. "The number is Son 224."[17]

In Eindhoven there is the 'Airborne Laan'. Here at the edge of a small ornamental garden arranged in the rather harsh Dutch fashion, but naturally exceedingly neat as the Dutch themselves are, there is a wooden sign with the 'Screaming Eagle' divisional patch of the 101st. It leads the way to a stone memorial with a schematic map of the Wilhelmina Canal and mentions of the Division's 502nd and 506th Regiments.

But after the 'Son Airborne Memorial' to the 101st at Son, which takes the form of a just landed airborne trooper with a grenade in his hand, ready to throw, the most poignant memorial to the 'Screaming Eagles' is that in the open air theatre at <u>Best</u>. It was erected by public subscription and pays tribute to the memory of a single member of the 101st Airborne Division.

It is the 'Joe Mann Memorial' to Private First Class Joe E. Mann, who gave his life for his comrades and won the Medal of Honor posthumously doing so. On 19th Sept. 1944 after a bridge there was blown, Mann and nineteen other troopers were cut off. We know what happened then and how Mann's self-sacrifice, the ultimate one, saved the lives of his fellow paras.

At first sight it seems a strange memorial to a soldier. It is that of a pelican! Four stone pillars support the bird sitting on the nest of her young with bas-relief figures portraying the stages of Joe Mann's gallantry. So why a pelican? The local artist who created it had fallen back on the old legend of the pelican who fed her young with her own blood: a symbol of self-sacrifice, in other words.

This kind of unusual symbolism is repeated at the 101st memorial at Veghel Airborne Memorial. This time it is in the form of a kangaroo with a baby in her pouch. The symbolism? It represents Allied airborne forces, jumping over the various Dutch rivers and canals. Close by there is a more conventional plaque commemorating Veghel's liberation by the 501 PIR on 17th September 1944. There are other reminders of the 'Screaming Eagles'. A local street named after Col. Howard Johnson, who commanded the 501st PIR (Johnsonlaan)... a

170

large brick building at the corner of the Johnsonlaan and the Hoogstraat - the High Street - which was used as the 'Screaming Eagles' HQ. On the top of the wrought iron gates to the place, which incorporate the words 'Klondyke', there is that familiar proud device, the 'Screaming Eagle' ...

It is a permanent reminder of the young men like Colonel Johnson 'Geronimo' who once came this way and paid the ultimate sacrifice ...

BASTOGNE II

Of all the places in which the 'Screaming Eagles' fought in Europe, not one is so well provided with tourist attractions and tangible memories of the terrible events of that year, 1944/45, than the Bastogne area. Here there are memorials to great events and obscure ones; to famous soldiers who will live on forever in military history and obscure ones who are remembered due to fate, mere chance.

Naturally the first step on this memory trail for the battlefield tourist tracing the flight of the 'Screaming Eagles' is at the grave of America's most famous (some would say most infamous) soldier of the campaign in Europe - General George S. Patton.

On leaving the capital of Luxembourg, head for the airport on the throughway. Just before you reach the place at the first roundabout at Hamm, you'll see the elongated red, white and blue marker announcing US Military Cemetery. Here to the front of graves which mark the passing of Patton's soldiers of the Third Army is the simple white grave of the 'boss' himself.

Once clear of the city's outskirts (Patton's HQ during the Battle was at the present old folks' home, the Pascatore Foundation, marked by a plaque). From here follow the road to Arlon (not the motorway but the 'N' roads). Here Patton started his relief attack for Bastogne. Here at Arlon there is a good Battle of the Bulge museum, well worth visiting. On to Bastogne northwards, using the main and parallel roads, both used by the US Fourth Armored Division. To your right you'll see the bunker (marked) where Boggess met the young airborne artillery officer.

Naturally 'Nuts City' (Bastogne) is one great memorial to the 101st Airborne, ranging from the Sherman tank and bust of McAuliffe in the main square to the great and most major Battle of the Bulge museum (the Historical Center) at the other end of the Belgian town. Here the true magnitude of America's 20th century Gettysburg, the Bulge, is symbolised by the monument recording the names of all the 76,850 Americans killed, wounded or reported missing during the six week struggle.[48]

On to Clervaux - the back road from the Historical Center - with its castle museum celebrating the sacrifice of the US 28th Infantry Division as von Luettwitz's corps headed for Bastogne, Diekirch with the Luxembourg National War Museum (again a must) and finally to Ettelbruck, where at the very awkward bend in the main road there is an American wartime Sherman tank with its gun pointing menacingly north, the way Patton attacked. Next to it is the statue[49] of 'Old Blood an' Guts'. He is dressed in a fur-collared, leather jacket and holding his binoculars, that familiar scowl on his 'war face' as he always called it. Currently some obscure protester has given the jacket a coat of red paint (for blood spilled in the Balkans). But that in no way detracts from the place of affection found in the hearts of the Luxembourgers, to whom he is a national hero!

One and all, they are frozen for all time thus in stone, metal and concrete, a fitting memorial to all those who fought and died at Bastogne - America's Screaming Eagles and those who felt they were rescuing them ...

ALSACE LORRANE
OPERATION NORTHWIND

Of all the battlefields over which the 101st Airborne Division fought in Allied countries during World War Two, that of Alsace Lorraine shows the least signs of their passing. Normandy, Holland, Belgium and Luxembourg display numerous mementos to the 'blood, sweat and tears' of those long dead paratroopers. They are remembered everywhere from humble plaques to great museums. Not in that border region of France. Perhaps it is due to the fact that it is close to the border and that, even today, many of the locals still speak a German dialect as their main language.

Here the French seem to have forgotten their debt of blood. All that remains of the 101st's month on the line of the River Moder are the shallow depressions in the woods which were once foxholes, or the odd mortar 'butterfly' bomb carrier with the date '1944' stamped in the crumbling rusty metal; the odd jerrican still being used by the local French dirt farmers with the British 'WD' (War Department) and official arrow on its side.

Now, who remembers that bold, desperate young men once passed this way today? Only at the big US military cemetery outside Epinal, where the dead of the Seventh Army are buried, does one remember. On that tree-covered hill site stretching as far as the eye can see are the white crosses and the occasional Star of David, in death as rigid as they were in life on parade. Dated January and February 1945, they bear mute testimony to America's sacrifice and those young men who died to liberate 'La Belle France'.

ENVOI

'Ya never had it so good' was the scornful cry from fellow GIs which had greeted the 'Eagles' throughout their career in the 101st Airborne. 'Hell, you guys have found a home in the Army'. The cry had been greeted with the 'Bronx cheer'[50] and a few salty comments. Now for once, the troopers who had fought so long and so hard could accept that scornful cry with equanimity. For a short while before the balloon went up again - there was still the 'Nips' to fight - they had found a nice comfortable billet in the US Army.

There was booze a-plenty and (for those who could speedily forget what they had seen the previous month at Landsberg) broads ('frats') too. The sun and scenery were like something out of a kid's fairy tale, as well. The Bavarian-Austrian border where the troopers now found themselves stationed was filled with imitation medieval castles (many had been built by prosperous Southern Germans in the late 19th century), overlooking idyllic still lakes, in which the snow-tipped Alps were reflected.

All the same, the pace of life in this once remote area was hectic. The supposed 'Alpine Redoubt', which Dulles of the OSS had invented, was packed with rogues, renegades and a wide assortment of rascals from half a dozen nationalities. There were wanted war criminals, using the 'ratlines' (as the escape routes were called) to vanish to South America; black-marketeers of all shapes and forms, wheeling and dealing in everything from penicillin to oil paintings; <u>Reichsbank</u> officials being chased by 'Safehaven'[51] teams, busy hiding their stolen gold and precious stones in the mountains before the Allied authorities caught up with them... In short, it was a crazy time.

But the days of wine and roses were speedily coming to an end. The two atomic bombs speedily ended Japan's participation in WWII and there would be no need for the 101st and its sister outfit, the 82nd, which it had been planned should drop on Tokyo's airports. General Maxwell left to become Superintendent of West Point and his men knew they wouldn't be going out to the Pacific as he had predicted. The younger troopers started being transferred to other outfits, in particular the 17th Airborne, which had jumped over the Rhine. The 'Screaming Eagles' predictably didn't like the transfer. The 101st's 'Art Gallery', that great collection of Old Masters, mostly stolen by 'Fat Hermann', as the Germans called Hermann Goering, the now imprisoned head of the Luftwaffe, was closed. The 'Golden Age', as the survivors called that summer, with fond memories, was about over.

On 30th November 1945, the 101st Airborne Division was deactivated in Auxerre, France. It had had an active life of nearly four years and had, as the now dead 'Father of the Airborne' had predicted back in 1942, 'blazed a trail across the skies'. But the war was over and people wanted to forget the fighting. Most of the veterans returned home without ceremony. A handful of the men, who had been transferred to its sister outfit, the 82nd Airborne, did march with that division down Fifth Avenue. But that was about it. They had come home, as they had departed, unheralded and unrecognised: just another bunch of GIs. But then that has always been the lot of combat soldiers once the battle has been won.

For another five years nothing was heard of the 'Screaming Eagles'. Then came Korea. In 1950, the 101st was reactivated as a training and holding division at Camp Breckenridge, Kentucky. Brigade-sized airborne operations and battles did take part in Korea. But the 101st stayed at home.

But now the world was changing. The new 'cold war' was threatening to turn into a 'hot war' anywhere on the globe. Rapid deployment forces such as presented by the airborne divisions, were needed in the US Army once more. In 1956 the 101st was re-activated as a fully-fledged airborne outfit at Fort Campbell, Kentucky, where it has been based ever since. The rest is, as they say, history.

Those young men who went off to war in Vietnam, the Gulf and a half a dozen minor conflicts elsewhere since have been worthy successors to the surviving veterans of the 'Old War': the men who can declare in, admittedly reedy, old men's voices, that once they fought in places such as 'Normandy... Holland... Bastogne... the Bitch Bulge... Berchtesgaden... the stuff that legends are made of.[52] After all these now frail, white-haired old men were the ones who captured Hitler's own lair – 'The Eagle's Nest"...

Naturally a defeated Germany would not raise any monuments to its conquerors and, there are no outward signs in Bavaria that the 'Screaming Eagles' passed this way to their final conquest at Berchtesgaden. But the battlefield tourist can still find traces enough of the way those once young men travelled if he wishes. Berchtesgaden and area is packed with mementos of that evil regime which they helped to destroy.

Come out of the little station at Berchtesgaden, for instance, and on the hill opposite the cemetery there are the graves of Hitler's half sister, Paula Hitler, and no less a person than Dr. Todt, the creator of the Siegfried Line and Atlantic Wall, which they had once attacked so long ago.

Above towers that 'birthday present' that the 'King of the Mountains', Martin Borman, gave to his Führer on the former's fiftieth birthday - the 'Eagle's Nest", But the birthday present can only be visited in the summer and only then by special bus. These are equipped with 280 HP engines and take twenty long minutes to cover the mere four miles from the parking lot at the base of the road to the top. It's not surprising, however. The bends are hairpin and, although the views from the windows of the bus are spectacular, they keep one's heart in one's mouth, as the local driver negotiates yet another bend. Have no fear gentle tourist; the bus company has had a one hundred per cent safety record from 1952 to the present!

Downhill on a twenty-seven per cent gradient, the brakes of the bus function automatically so the driver doesn't even need to apply his foot brake pedal. Still there are still those nervous souls who whisper a fervent prayer of gratitude once they're down at the parking lot once more.

Upon arriving at the tunnel which leads to the 'Eagle's Nest", visitors have to line up to have their tickets stamped with their time of departure. While you wait look at the brass door of the entrance. You might note that something seems to be missing. There is. Two massive lion-shaped door handles. One is in the hands of an American private collector. The other is in the possession of no less than the family of the former commander of the Allied wartime armies in Europe - President Dwight D. Eisenhower!

Back in 1951, when the Germans were making their first attempts to re-assert themselves after their terrible defeat in the war, one of the prices they had to pay for being admitted to the 'Mountain' once more was the destruction of the 'big shots' homes, or what was left of them.

This was duly done and the local Bavarian authorities ordered that quick-growing trees should be planted on these sites. These were planted some seven feet apart so that thickets were swiftly produced to hide the tumbled stones and make access to these extremely difficult. No one was going to set up memorials to the dead, as would be tried in the graveyard where Hess, Bormann's former boss, was to be buried. Time and Nature have played their part. Today, fifty years on, very few of even the locals recall where the surviving stones are located, save in one case.

This is just off the road that leads upwards to the Eagle's Nest'. Here there is a rough and ready, muddy parking spot, perhaps only large enough for two cars to park. Not that many people want to park there, for the place stinks! The reason is simple. For it is here that dog-owners visiting the Nazi sites usually allow their darling pets to 'relieve themselves', as they put it delicately.

In yet another supreme irony of recent German history, the home of the once all-powerful 'King of the Mountain', Martin Bormann, is now remembered solely as a good place where 'Wau-Wau kann pinkeln' (doggie can take a pee).

As the Roman poet Juvenal put it aptly about allegedly great men and their fate nearly two thousand years ago now: 'The bad jokes of Fortune. Village pierrots yesterday, arbiters of life and death today, tomorrow keepers of the public latrines'.

How true... how true ...

ENDNOTES

[1] In essence President Clinton was booed by the veterans of the Ranger battalions when he spoke to them on the anniversary, while the veteran of the US 10th Mountain Division, badly wounded in the fighting of Italy, Senator Dole, was roundly cheered.

[2] In Belgium three languages are spoken: French, Flemish and German.

[3] He was shot by mistake by an SS trooper.

[4] Warned by a top secret Ultra signal. Thus Gen. Freyburg was not allowed to alter his dispositions to meet the German air raid attack in case he gave away the great secret.

[5] They would go to North Africa with the 'Red Devils' wearing that famed red beret and some of them still wearing it - <u>against orders</u> - two years later.

[6] Officers received one hundred dollars a month; enlisted men fifty; a sizeable amount in those days.

[7] This was the only uniform on board the ship which rescued him that would fit him. A month later he was killed in action in the fighting in Italy. The first Allied airborne General to be killed on the battlefield. Brigadier General Pratt, Asst. Div. Commander of the 101st AB was the next, on 6th June 1944, Normandy.

[8] A year later when the same Regiment dropped a battalion over another island, chaos ensued just as at Sicily: friendly fire, panicked pilots and a third wave dropped into the ocean. But no-one ever learned about that op.

[9] For those of a genteel nature, we shall use a euphemism for this popular phrase of those long ago years when young men about to die were not particularly mealy-mouthed, '<u>Mucked Up Beyond All Recognition</u>' will have to suffice.

[10] There were several cases of men disappearing on the battlefield only to report in several months later. One Sergeant even managed to wangle his way as a 'prison guard' on a ship taking POWs back to the States. But on the whole the 'Screaming Eagles' did all that was expected from them and paid the 'butcher's bill' accordingly.

[11] Jagdbomber

[12] Ironically many of the defensives and weapons, including Renault tanks, used by the Germans on the beaches to stop France's 'liberators' were of French manufacture or origin.

[13] "Market' was the airborne operation; 'Garden', the ground assault.

[14] Since the war there has been much talk that a Dutch double agent, nicknamed (for obvious reasons) 'King Kong', betrayed the

Allied plan in advance to the Germans. However, the German spymaster who ran 'King Kong', Major Giskes, assured the author that this wasn't the case. It was just unfortunate that two SS Panzer divisions (the presence of which he Allies knew) were in the area of the Arnhem landings.

[15] In training British infantrymen always carried a full water-bottle, but it was commonplace to march twenty miles before the officer in charge of a route-march gave permission to take a drink from the water-bottle.

[16] Just like the Americans couldn't seem to get along with the 'Limeys', the latter had similar reservations about the 'Yanks'. The author's own division, 52nd Lowland, came under 101st command for a while during the battle in the 'Corridor', but it wasn't very successful.

[17] Later a Major Thomas, commanding the British engineers, did this and was connected with Gen. Taylor, courtesy of the German telephone switchboard!

[18] Heaped up earth to form a ford a foot or so beneath the surface of the water.

[19] At Bastogne, one can be in four other European countries within the hour.

[20] One day later, 20th December, a messenger from Patton's intelligence was carrying his plan of attack to Bradley's HQ hidden in a champagne bottle in his jeep attached to a can of gas, just in case he had to burn the plan. It is clear that the Plan was not so impromptu as historians at the time thought.

[21] The German version of this ultimatum survives; the English version has vanished. As one of the most celebrated messages in US military history, it would bring a fortune if it were re-discovered today.

[22] There is a sombre picture extant of a US paratrooper turning away sorry-looking Belgian civilians at the perimeter because there were no rations available to feed them inside Bastogne. In the picture the crestfallen civilians turn back to face the no-man's land and its dangers.

[23] i.e of the Fourth Armored

[24] Colonel Abrams and Colonel Cohen, commanders of the 37th Tank and 10th Armored Infantry Battalions were both Jewish.

[25] General Patch's Seventh Army had taken over this sector after Patton's Third Army had moved north to counter-attack into the 'Bulge'.

[26]

[27] Devers was in command of the US 6th Army Group to which the US 7th Army belonged. Eisenhower had had several run-ins with Devers in 43/44 and disliked him intensely. Indeed at the

end of the war when the Supreme Commander was asked by Washington to rate his commanders, Devers came way down his list, even lower, in some cases, than mere corps commanders.

28   After Patton was dismissed from the 7th Army, it never succeeded in getting a commander who was capable of obtaining publicity as he had always been able to in Sicily.

29   The 36th felt that they had been unnecessarily slaughtered at the crossing of the River Rapido.

30   According to her own self-seeking accounts.

31   Eclipse was basically a plan for taking over the admin. of Hitler's Germany in case of a sudden collapse. It also, however, envisaged 'Operation Talisman', an airdrop on Berlin by Ridgway's XVIII AB Corps. The Allies thought the plan was secret. But the Germans had had a copy since January 1945. Gavin told the author he thought the Russians had slipped the plan to the Germans for their own nefarious purposes.

32   Eisenhower had decreed that troops would only speak to children under the age of ten. Any adult German could be only spoken to on official business. 'Yeah, monkey business,' the troops quipped, especially if the 'German adult' was a buxom blonde.

33   His body was found after ten years, was secretly conveyed to the German War Cemetery at Vossenach in the Hurtgen, where it was 'stolen' a few years ago now. It is still missing. Curious.

34   'Fratting', as it was called, had its consequences, of course. In a year there were 30,000 illegitimate German children born as a consequence of these illicit relationships.

35   'Ducks' were really DUKWs - all-wheel drive vehicle which could carry twenty troopers in comfort and buzz along at fifty miles an hour, even on the battle-pitted German roads, due to their oversized rubber tyres.

36   Hitler remained an Austrian citizen until 1928.

37   Hitler's royalties for <u>Mein Kampf</u> continued until well after his death in 1945, but the author has been unable to find a figure for year 2000.

38   Fritz Lang, the refugee German film director, gives some idea of the place in his acclaimed fictional thriller '<u>The Man Hunt</u>' (1941).

39   Brown because the original Party uniform had been brown, giving birth to the members' name of 'brownshirts'.

40   Literally 'under four eyes', i.e. privately.

41   Even in the Nazis' vaunted 'workers' state', great importance was paid to academic titles, just as it is today when snobbish Germans pay enormous sums for doctors' titles from obscure non-German universities.

42   Crudely, 'pleasure in other people's misfortune'.

43   <u>Vegeltungswaffen</u>', i.e. revenge weapon.

44   After its stand on the French River Marne in WWI.

45   LeClerc had been sentenced to death by the Vichy Government for taking up arms under de Gaulle back in 1940.

46   In a footnote in the book, Butcher, who was Eisenhower's PA, first mentioned the disaster at Slapton.

47   Because the divisional patch has the shape of a red bucket.

48   British visitors will undoubtedly be saddened by the absence of the 2,600 British names: the number of casualties that the British Army suffered south of Bastogne. Once again the British Army is apparently a forgotten army.

49   The same statue is also at West Point

50   For the British reader - a raspberry.

51   <u>Safehaven</u> was used, in part by the Allies to recover stolen Allied goods and, more importantly, ensure that the Nazi loot from a German-dominated Europe of the War should be restored. As we know, the US authorities, in particular, are still battling on that score while the victims who might benefit die daily in their scores nearly sixty years later.

52   This year the 101st hosted the major sixtieth anniversary of the foundation of the US parachute corps in June 1940.

INDEX